Y0-AGT-855

A NEW SCIENCE
OF STOCK MARKET
INVESTING

How to Predict Stock
Price Movements
Consistently and Profitably

A NEW SCIENCE OF STOCK MARKET INVESTING

How to Predict Stock Price Movements Consistently and Profitably

GERALD H. ROSEN
M. R. Wehr Professor Emeritus
Drexel University

1817

Harper & Row, Publishers, New York
BALLINGER DIVISION

Grand Rapids, Philadelphia, St. Louis, San Francisco
London, Singapore, Sydney, Tokyo, Toronto

Copyright © 1990 Gerald Harris Rosen. All rights reserved.
No part of this publication may be reproduced, stored in a retrieval system,
or transmitted in any form or by any means, electronic, mechanical,
photocopy, recording, or otherwise, without the prior written consent of
the publisher and the author.

While the method of stock investment described in this book is believed to
be reliably efficient, there is no guarantee that the method will be profitable
in specific applications, owing to the risk that is always inherent in any
stock investment. Thus, neither the publisher nor the author can assume
liability for any loss that may be sustained by use of the method described
in this book, and any such liability is hereby expressly disclaimed. The
author and the publisher are not engaged in rendering legal, accounting,
or other professional advice for which the reader is advised to seek the
services of a qualified professional.

International Standard Book Number: 0-88730-393-5

Library of Congress Catalog Card Number: 89-24512

Printed in the United States of America

Library of Congress Cataloging-in-Publication Data

Rosen, Gerald H. (Gerald Harris), 1933-
    A new science of stock market investing : how to predict stock price
movements consistently and profitably / Gerald H. Rosen.
        p. cm.
    ISBN 0-88730-393-5
    1. Stock–Prices. 2. Investments. 3. Speculation. I. Title
HG4636.R67   1988
332.63′22–dc20   89-24512
                                                              CIP

90 91 92 93 HD 9 8 7 6 5 4 3 2 1

For my mother, Shirley Rosen,
for my children Lawrence and Karlyn,
and for all those who share
a similar predilection for independence

Defendit numerus [there is safety in crowds]
is the maxim of the foolish;
deperdit numerus [there is ruin in crowds]
of the wise.

–Charles C. Colton

CONTENTS

ILLUSTRATIONS AND TABLES

PREFACE

Way back in the 'Twenties there was
a successful trader named William
D. Gann who authored a book in
which he offered "advice in the science of speculation and investment
in the same spirit as the physician."
When I discovered a copy of Gann's
book in the attic at home before
going to college, I hardly supposed
that I would ever present "advice
in the science of investment and
trading in the spirit of a theoretical physicist." Now, however, the
institutional *Octoberfest* of 1987 has
made it very evident that the passive and compliant method of making buy, hold and sell decisions on
the basis of fundamental and technical analysis provided by professional "experts" (full-service brokerage firms and advisory services) is at
best unreliable and inefficient and at
worst can make the user a *fall guy*

*artful advice on
the science of
equity investing*

to fest or to fall

*"Always the
Gods give . . . .
things to the
small." –
Callimachus*

*a farewell to
nonsense*

of the *fest*. Owing to the dominant presence of institutional money managers who enjoy a special alliance with security analysts, have immediate access to fresh information, and are equipped to trade large blocks of stocks rapidly, the independent private investor has to compete in a rather hostile environment. But on the other hand, like the fighter aircraft that had so much success in combat with the much larger well-armed bombers of World War II, the independent private investor has the basic advantages that go with smallness and mobility. Combined with the necessary amount of market sophistication provided by the findings in this book, smallness and mobility can indeed enable the individual investor to markedly outperform the institutions on a consistent basis.

The purpose and contents of this book are quite different from previous literature on the stock market. With the objective of achieving more than just parity for the individual private investor, I have attempted to make this book incisive, concise and absolutely free of notions which are not productively useful in practice. The primary goal has been to provide an accurate and detailed description of the degree of predictability associated with stock price movements, for an understanding of this fascinating subject is the key to superior results with stock investments. Essentially based on a comprehensive study of insider transactions and P-V (price-volume) graphs, the new material presented in this book leads to an eminently sound method for making profitable stock investments with relatively low risk, as described in the final chapter.

concentrating on what is predictable for superior results

In essence, the superior method for stock investments that follows from the price-predictability findings involves a synergistic multi-component screening, selecting and monitoring procedure for purchase candidates and holdings. One starts with the legally reported data on insider buying (information published monthly by the federal government) and applies a filter that selects the stocks with the highest *a priori* probability of major price appreciation from all those with significant *i*nsider *b*uying, abbreviated *sib*. A stock in the latter category, referred to as *sib*+, is either P-V bullish or P-V bearish at any time, as indicated in a mathematically precise and unambiguous fashion by

putting it all together

the essential synergism: sib+ and positive P-V graphics

its P-V graph. Additional practical tenets are employed along with P-V graphs to facilitate the purchasing, efficient monitoring, and eventual sale of holdings at logically appropriate price levels. With patient adherence to the method, one can achieve a consistently high level of success with stock investments in all phases of the economic cycle.

"Experience is the name everyone gives to his or her mistakes."
–Wilde

I have endeavored to make this book readily understandable to those who are just beginning with stocks, as well as valuable to investors with all levels of experience. As with a corporate annual report, the subordinate material that appears in the footnotes should be read sooner or later. In particular, the references cited in footnotes have been carefully selected to provide further important insights. However, as in any other competitive activity, there is no substitute for actual involvement and experience at doing it.

"Skill to do comes of doing."
–Emerson

What should the user of this method for stock investment expect to achieve over longer-term time frames? I have employed the method described in the final chapter of this book with excellent results over the past sixteen years. An average net investment return equal to about twice the percentile gain in the Dow is usually attainable during multi-month holding periods when the Dow advances, as illustrated in a fairly typical manner by the detailed example in the Appendix. Moreover, by adherence to the method, the greater part of the user's investment assets will ordinarily be out of the market and in cash equivalents prior to a major decline in the Dow. (This was the case for my investments by mid-1987, and I did not own a single share of stock on October 19, 1987.) Thus, on the basis of my personal experience, a user of the method should expect to achieve very positive results during periods of Dow bull markets and more modest results with preservation of investment capital during periods of Dow bear markets.

outperforming the Dow

timely exits before declines

The centrally important and numerous contributions made to this book by my wife and investment partner, Sarah, are gratefully acknowledged. Our daughter Karlyn also assisted with Figures 2,3, the illustrations on pages 18 and 155, and some up-to-date computer expertise. Finally, I am indebted to Mark Greenberg and Martha Jewett at Harper & Row for their enthusi-

thanks to family helpers and Harper & Row professionals

astic interest and their perspicacious suggestions for refinements in the original manuscript. The rest was easy!

GHR

1

ELEMENTS OF A PARADIGM FOR PREDICTABILITY

In *Annie Hall* Woody Allen remarks, "Everything our parents said was good is bad: sun, milk, red meat, college. . . . " My first exposure to stock market research at college was actually bad and good: on the one hand it emphasized the random walk theory, with the exclusion of practically everything else, but on the other hand it inculcated a healthy skepticism about stock movement predictability and price-based trad-

getting
brainwashed

1

ing systems. Entitled *Speculative Security Markets*, this special one-term elective presented elaborate statistical evidence that stock price movements were essentially random and unpredictable.[1] However, the statistical evidence came exclusively from time-series of stock prices, without regard for the associated trading volume or the fundamental factors that possibly may have influenced future price changes. The absence of significant correlations between successive price changes in daily, weekly, and monthly time-series for large numbers of stocks indicated that a useful signal for predicting future price movement did not exist simply in the record of past prices.

Many of us who had signed up for this special course had hoped to learn how John Maynard Keynes, Bernard Baruch, and other successful stock market personages had operated from year to year in a reliably profitable fashion. Disappointed by this "no-go" view of stock price predictability, a sarcastic guy in the back of the lecture hall asked, "Were Lord Keynes and Bernard Baruch fictional characters?" Meanwhile, I

the fly in the ointment

"A protest—only a bubble in the molten mass— pops and sighs out, and the mass hardens."
—R. Jeffers

"Okay, if there's no God, who changes the water?"

Gerald Rosen. from The Princeton Tiger. copyright 1955

vented my frustration in not learning anything useful about stock price
movement by sketching a cartoon,
reproduced here as memorabilia.

My indoctrination that *stock prices
move in an unpredictable random
fashion* was further reinforced by
an article in the *Princeton Alumni
Weekly* (April 25, 1972). Apparently
irrefutable statistical evidence had
now been compiled and analyzed

at Princeton's Center for Financial Research by R. E. Quandt, B. G. Malkiel, and W. J. Baumol.[2] These researchers at the Center, called a "menace" by Value Line in a one-third page rebuttal ad in the *New York Times*, had shown that the traditional approach based on fundamental and technical analysis was "simply no help to investors at all" and one could probably do better by merely "throwing darts" at a page of corporate names. This at least suggested a possible explanation for Lord Keynes—skill learned with darts at his local pub—but what about Baruch?

"Love truth, but pardon error."
—Voltaire

Being risk averse and not having a trustworthy set of darts, I was interested in learning some other stock market paradigm. One day at lunch a finance professor told me about the α and β introduced by W. F. Sharpe[3] in his equation

Sharpe's equation

$$\ln P = \alpha + \beta \ln P_M$$

where ln is the natural logarithm, P is the time-varying expected price of a certain stock, P_M is the time-varying "price of the market" (represented by an index like the Dow-Jones Industrial Average—the

"Dow"), and α and β (the latter now "beta" in advisory service stock reports and defined to be constant) are quantities associated with the stock. In principle, Sharpe's equation transfers the problem of individual stock price predictability to general stock market predictability in cases for which α remains constant—a rather stringent assumption in practice. I left lunch with the feeling that predicting α and P_M was seemingly more difficult than predicting P directly, and therefore I still wanted to learn some other paradigm.

indigestion

Sharpe's equation actually reminded me of the empirical finding by Johannes Kepler in 1617. As a precursor to the development of quantitative physics, Kepler observed that the mean distances from the sun D and periods of revolution around the sun T were related in the same mathematical way for all six known planets (see Table 1 on p. 6). In Sharpe's format, the Keplerian planetary relation is

the inner preoccupations of a physicist's mind

$$\ln D = \alpha + \beta \ln T$$

Kepler's equation

where $\alpha = 0.599$ and $\beta = \frac{2}{3}$. Isaac Newton accounted for the Keplerian

Table 1.   D and T for the Orbits of the Six
Innermost Planets

The Sharpe-like Keplerian relation $\ln D = \alpha + \beta \ln T$ is satisfied by the pair of D, T values in the table for each planet, with $\alpha = 0.599$ and $\beta = \frac{2}{3}$. In the Sharpe equation itself for average price correlation, D is replaced by P and T is replaced by P_M.

	D, *Mean Distance from the Sun (millions of miles)*	T, *Period of Revolution around Sun (earth days)*
Mercury	36.0	88.0
Venus	67.3	224.7
Earth	93.0	365.2
Mars	141.7	687
Jupiter	483.7	4332
Saturn	887.1	10759

relation and $\beta = \frac{2}{3}$ theoretically, in the context of classical mechanics with gravitational motion, in his *Principia* (1687). However, during the seventy years between Kepler's and Newton's publications, a number of *cargo cult notions* were popularized by others to explain the D, T planetary relation.

A *cargo cult notion*, an expression coined by the physicist R. P. Feynman,[4] refers to a popularized belief that ignores an essentially important aspect of the problem and thus does not yield a practical payoff. The airstrip on a South Pacific island had been abandoned shortly after World War II, and cargo planes no longer landed with Spam and canned fruit cocktail. Motivated by a desire to bring back the cargo, the natives did some thinking. They observed that the tower next to the airstrip had been removed, and they conjectured (quite correctly) that a tower was necessary in order for cargo planes to land. However, no planes landed even after the natives had implemented their notion by building a new tower of bamboo.

"Every person take the limits of his or her vision for the limits of the world."
—Schopenhauer

While cargo cult notions do not survive very long in the realm of science, they are alive and flourishing elsewhere. Hence it was erroneous to suppose that the logical place to find a useful stock market paradigm would be in a library. After much searching, cross-referencing, xeroxing, and reading over an extended period of time, I became convinced that a practical and efficient paradigm was not to be found in the existing literature. The subject of stock market trading systems was in fact a fertile field for cargo cultists, and their works, conventionally titled something like

bookworming

"How to Get Rich ... in the Stock Market", frequently turned up in public libraries, either donated by the publisher or by a disillusioned user. At the more learned opposite extreme in university libraries, the paramount problem of individual stock price predictability was sidestepped by scholarly authors,[5] who simply advocated the broad diversification of one's holdings and a basic buy-and-hold strategy. This prevailing stock market paradigm, maintained by most academicians circa 1970 to the present, derived from the repeated failures of price-based trading schemes to work efficiently in practice.[6] Prior to the Crash in October 1987, the diversification paradigm continued to be in vogue for large-scale investors such as portfolio managers—especially ones with more cash to invest than free time to be selective.

Of course, diversification and basic passivity (buy, hold, and pray) never made any sense for the small independent investor, who, while having less access to information pertinent to corporate prospects, has the compensating advantage of being able to buy and sell stocks very selectively without committee approval or sig-

"No one is exempt from talking nonsense; the misfortune is to do it solemnly.'
—Montaigne

the quick and easy way to go

the need to focus

nificant price impact. Moreover, the strategic principle of concentration of forces, which works so well in most forms of competitive activity, runs counter to the concept of diversification. Because it takes more time and effort to monitor a large number of stocks than to concentrate attention and investment capital on one or a few that offer the best prospects, diversification often produces comparatively mediocre results.

A satisfactory paradigm for stock market investing only emerged after I had considered the literature, critically discounted the cargo cult notions, and then performed my own studies on the relevancy of various forms of available information for future stock price movement. I became interested in learning more about legally reported insider transactions and how they might contribute to stock price predictability. This subject is discussed in Chapter II. The main finding in my study of insider transactions is that this information is useful for predicting the price movements of the more visible, actively traded New York Stock Exchange (NYSE) issues with satisfactory investment qual-

legally reported insider transactions

concentrating on the NYSE stocks with visibility and investment quality

ity, where "visibility" here admits an unambiguous practical definition. On the other hand, legally reported insider buying is very often misleading when it pertains to the more obscure and lower quality NYSE stocks or to issues that are not listed on the NYSE.

P-V graphics

I also investigated ways of circumventing the statistical evidence for unpredictability that was based on time-series of past prices.[1,2] Because even well-known stocks have periods of relatively quiet dullness with modest daily volume followed by periods of lively activity with large daily volume, a part of the sporadic randomness or "noise" in the time-series of a stock's price could be due to the stochastic variability in its trading volume from day to day, from week to week, and from month to month. Therefore, to obtain a more meaningful signal with less "noise," it seemed logical to graph a stock price P as a quantity dependent on *cumulative volume* V, the total number of shares traded up to the time of interest, rather than as a quantity dependent on time. It soon became clear that some of the unpredictability in stock price movement (when price is expressed as a function of time, as on most charts) did indeed derive from the unpredictable variation of daily, weekly, and monthly volume with time. This degree of unpredictability is automatically eliminated by considering price as a quantity dependent on cumulative volume.

Figure 1 on p. 12 is an illustrative P-V graph showing the price P (dollars per share) versus cumulative volume V (millions of shares traded) for AT&T common stock from 1/4/88 through 1/22/88. Weekly volume and price figures, obtained from a Sunday newspaper or a financial weekly, appear above the figure. Observe that a continuous segmented straight line approximation for P is employed in such a P-V graph, running with a piecewise-constant slope from a week's close, to the subsequent week's high (or low), to the week's low (or high), and finally to the week's close. The logical interpretation and practical utility of P-V graphs is discussed along with examples in Chapter III. In addition to signalling the onset of major up or down price movements in their early stages, P-V graphs

constructing a P-V graph

Figure 1. Illustrative P-V graph showing price P versus cumulative volume V for AT&T common stock during indicated three week period. Price-volume data:

	Sales 100's	High	Low	Close	Change
1/4/88–1/8/88	84829	$29\frac{3}{8}$	$27\frac{1}{4}$	$27\frac{3}{4}$	$+\frac{3}{4}$
1/11/88–1/15/88	97457	$29\frac{1}{8}$	$26\frac{3}{4}$	$29\frac{1}{8}$	$+1\frac{3}{8}$
1/18/88–1/22/88	61258	$29\frac{3}{8}$	$27\frac{1}{4}$	28	$-1\frac{1}{8}$

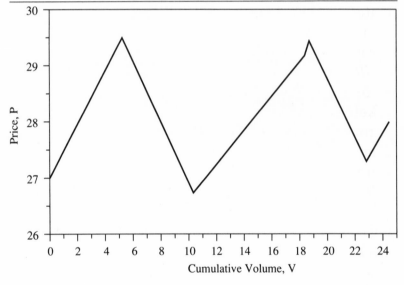

serve to classify the stock's regime of motion, based on the following hydrodynamic analogy.

a watched pot before it boils

If one heats a pot of water on a stove, the fluid motion can be observed to pass through a sequence of qualitatively distinct dynamical regimes. Two groupings of physical parameters, called the Rayleigh number and the Nusselt number, characterize the state of fluid motion at any instant of time. As shown in Figure 2 on p. 14 (from Khurana[7]), the Rayleigh and Nusselt numbers are well-correlated, with the fluid states lying along a curved line in the graph, as the fluid passes through the regimes of *convection, oscillation, chaos, transition, soft turbulence,* and *hard turbulence.* Likewise a stock has analogous regimes of motion, as described in Chapter III. Shown in Figure 1, the state of saw-tooth *oscillation* that AT&T's P-V graph exhibited during the first three weeks of 1988 (indicating a purely neutral condition for the stock, by up-down symmetry) is in marked contrast to its state of *hard turbulence* in October 1987.

"The solid angularity of facts."
—Emerson

The intermediate regime of *chaos* is the state of motion that usually characterizes a stock if the prospects for the company are clouded by major uncertainties. In the present context, *chaos* is not exactly what one finds in Webster's Dictionary, "a state of utter confusion," or what

Figure 2. Rayleigh-Nusselt number correlation and regimes of motion for a typical confined fluid [from Khurana (1988)].

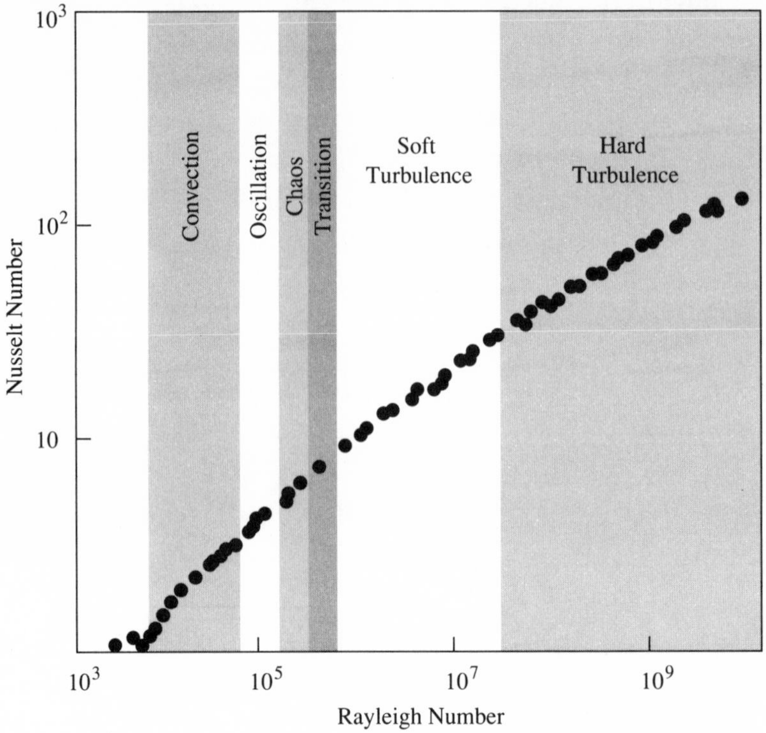

Alexander Pope had in mind when he wrote:

A work where nothing's just or fit;
One glaring chaos and heap of wit.

"While the mind is in doubt it is driven this way and that by a slight impulse."
—Terence

Rather, *chaos* refers to an erratic, aperiodic and stochastic (meaning randomlike) motion of a nonlinear system[8] governed by dynamical laws.[9] An example of *chaos*

Figure 3.   Energy versus number of pulses for a typical nonlinear system in a stochastic state of *chaos* [from Hogg and Huberman (1984)].

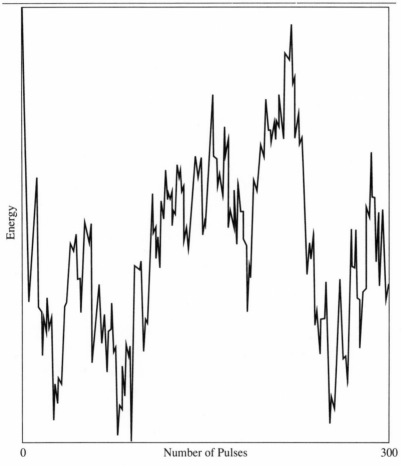

for a typical nonlinear system is shown in Figure 3 (from Hogg and Huberman[10]). A very similar form of *chaos* is exhibited by the P-V graph of LNF (Lomas & Nettleton Finan-

Figure 4.   LNF from 2/1/88 to 7/8/88 (ΔV = 42.8 from 39¼ to 15).

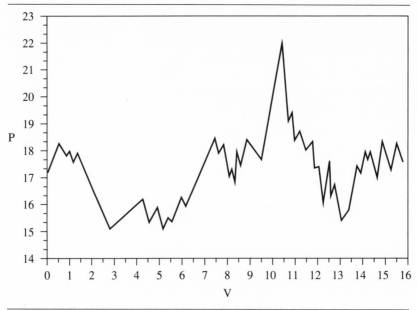

cial) from 2/1/88 to 7/8/88, shown here as Figure 4. In fact, if the *chaos* in LNF (associated with a P-V bearish condition, as described in Chapter III) were presented on a P-V graph based on daily rather than weekly price-volume data, the correspondence with Figure 3 would be even more striking.

Our paradigm also requires a number of additional practical tenets discussed in Chapter IV. The buying and selling by corporate insiders and what shows up on P-V graphs is only part of the story, for *imagery* and *informational asymmetry* often play important roles in influencing stock price movements. All too frequently it is a game played with free-flowing misinformation and concealed cards, and the truth regarding a company's prospects must be deduced from what is *not* reported to the financial media and shareholders. One must culture a skepticism and wariness about public pronouncements, propaganda, and market oracles. One must be able to draw inferences from the recommendations to buy, hold, or sell by security analysts, brokerage firms, and advisory services, recommendations which often stem from the *analyst-institution symbiosis* discussed in Chapter IV. Finally, one must always bear in mind the somewhat diabolical feature of an auction market: when you have a buy order executed, it means that you have paid more for the stock than anyone else is willing to pay at the time of purchase; when you have a sell order executed, it means that you have received less for the stock than anyone else is willing to accept at the time of sale. In either case, if your decision to buy or to sell is right, it implies that many

"Vast and varied misinformation."
—W. Gaynor

"You must wear your rue with a difference."
—Shakespeare

"I'd put a *sell* on this *dog* if I hadn't convinced the funds and banks to load up on it last month."

other participants in the market are wrong. You must be able to understand why they are wrong by seeing through imagery and sensing informational asymmetry.

Based on the predictable characteristics of stock price movements, Chapter 5 describes a method for screening and selecting stocks which have the highest expected total return subject to a minimal associated risk, purchasing such stocks at favorable price levels, and monitoring their subsequent price movements. The principal tools employed in this method are the legally reported insider transactions and P-V graphs of price versus cumulative volume, with appropriate logical interpretations. These tools must be buttressed by the additional practical tenets of the preceding paragraph and Chapter 4. One thereby arrives at a reliable and efficient method for achieving substantial profits in common stocks with relatively low risk.

"That ye may be perfect and entire, wanting nothing."
—Bible

NOTES

1. Some years later the random walk theory was described in greater detail by Granger, Clive and Oskar Morgenstern in *Predictability of Stock Prices*. New York: Heath Lexington, 1970. It is noteworthy that on p. 91 these authors remark, "It has not been proved that there exists no method that can produce useful investment predictions. . . . It is conceivable that a method which does not attempt to explain all movements but only a few more important ones could be successful . . . ," and on p. 96 they state, "whether or not future prices can be predicted using all available information (and not just price history) is a much wider question" (not addressed by random walk theory).
2. For a review of these findings, see Malkiel, Burton G., *A Random Walk Down Wall Street*. New York: Norton, 1973.

3. Sharpe, William F., "A Simplified Model for Portfolio Analysis," *Management Science*, Jan. 1963, pp. 277–293.
4. Feynman, Richard P., *Surely You're Joking, Mr. Feynman!* New York: Norton, 1985.
5. For example, see Clark, Jack C., and Stephen H. Archer, *Portfolio Analysis*. Englewood Cliffs, NJ: Prentice-Hall, 1971; Maginn, John L. and Donald L. Tuttle, *Managing Investment Portfolios*. New York: Warren, Gorham & Lamont, 1983, update 1985.
6. For example, see Fama, E., "Efficient Capital Markets: A Review of Theory and Empirical Work," *Journal of Finance*, May 1970, pp. 383–417.
7. Khurana, Anil, "Rayleigh-Bénard Experiment Probes Transition from Chaos to Turbulence." *Physics Today*, Vol. 41, June 1988, pp. 17–21.
8. For excellent introductions to the theory of *chaos*, see Eckmann, J. P., "Roads to Turbulence in Dissipative Dynamical Systems", *Review of Modern Physics*, Vol. 53, 1981, pp. 643–654; Ott, Edward, "Strange Attractors and Chaotic Motions of Dynamical Systems," ibid., pp. 655–671.
9. The motions of a *linear* system, like a violin string, can be superimposed to produce other admissible motions. A *nonlinear* system does not have solutions that are the superposition of other solutions. Almost all dynamical systems are nonlinear.
10. Hogg, T., and B. A. Huberman, "Chaos in the Classical Limit of Quantum Systems." *Physica Scripta*, Vol. 30, 1984, pp. 225–227.

2

LEGALLY REPORTED INSIDER TRANSACTIONS

When I picked up *Barron's* recently and came to an article entitled "The Smart Money,"[1] about how legally reported insider trading data can be useful as an aid in predicting future stock price movements, it was an echo from the past. I had first learned about the usefulness of legally reported insider trading data sixteen years earlier from a book[2] with the same title as the *Barron's* article but not men-

"Smart Money"?
Not always.

tioned in it. Detailed studies on the predictive characteristics of such insider trading data were actually performed by several authors in the 'Sixties.[3] While no citation exists in the literature surveyed by me, it is not entirely unlikely that the subject was first investigated much earlier, perhaps by an unknown professor of finance in the late 'Thirties when the Depression made publishers spurn manuscripts about stocks if not authored by Keynes or Baruch.

"Nothing is secret that shall not be made manifest."
—Bible

As a consequence of the Securities Exchange Act of 1934, insider buy and sell transactions must be reported to the federal government by the 10th of the month following the trade. Here and whenever the term is used in this book, *insider* refers to the officers, directors, principal security holders ("principal" meaning more than 10% of the shares outstanding), and affiliated persons (such as investment advisers) who are also required by the Act of 1934 to report their stock transactions to the Securities and Exchange Commission. Although lateness in reporting transactions is not uncommon, the essential compliance by officers, directors, and principal security holders has always been excellent.[4] Hopefully, the insider trading legislation of 1988 will promote a higher degree of compliance by affiliated persons.[5]

No one can doubt that insiders possess a unique perspective on important developments pertinent to the future of their company. Such developments may of course include projected higher earnings or an anticipated dividend increase; new products, inventions, and successful marketing or management techniques will also generally be known first to the insiders. The likelihood of future merger or tender offers, or important acquisitions, will become evident to the insiders well in advance of the actual occurrence. Moreover, it is the insiders who are best able to gauge the probability of a particular happening that may or may not impact the company importantly, in either a positive or a negative fashion.

insider perspective

If several insiders have elected to compound their vested interest in the company by putting a large investment of their personal savings "in the same basket" with open market stock purchases, it usually sig-

insider fallibility

nifies a weighty business decision. But do corporate insiders always make the right decision when they buy or sell their company's stock in the open market? Definitely not, and this fact has produced a long-standing dichotomy of opinion regarding the usefulness of tracking the insiders. In an article that appeared in the *Wall Street Journal*,[6] six knowledgeable individuals commented on the usefulness of insider trading information. Three of the individuals understood that this information could be very useful, while the other three expressed reservations. The *WSJ* article states:

the need to screen efficiently

"Even proponents ... concede that the raw data on insider purchases and sales is plagued by a number of problems." The main problem is that some of the data is basically misleading, reported by insiders who apparently[7] do not make the right decisions. Fortunately, such misleading data is easily eliminated in an efficient manner by the screening procedure described in this chapter.

Official Summary

After the Securities and Exchange Commission receives and compiles insider transaction data, it is published in monthly installments by the Government Printing Office in a periodical entitled *Official Summary of Security Transactions and Holdings,* or called *Official Summary* for short.[8] Volume 54 of *Official Summary* covers transactions reported in 1988 (since 1934 + 54 = 1988), and the monthly issues of each volume are numbered from 1 to 12. Personal computers and online databases now make it possible to receive some of this data more rapidly, but the isolated bits of insider buying and selling information in newspapers and financial magazines are too sketchy and incomplete to be used in a systematic and reliable fashion.

Time delays are of course involved in the reporting, compiling, publishing and mailing of the insider buy and sell information in *Official Summary.* The monthly issues of Volumes 53 and 54 of *Official Summary* showed an unusual variability in this time delay, as indicated by the dates in Table 2 on p. 26.

time delays in learning about insider transactions

In view of the reception dates for subscribers shown in Table 2, the average time delay involved in

Table 2. Dates Associated with *Official Summary* Volumes 53 and 54

Issue Number	Period in which transactions were reported to the SEC	Approximate date on which subscribers received Official Summary
1	12/11/86–1/12/87	4/16/87
2	1/13–2/10	5/21
3	2/11–3/10	6/19
4	3/11–4/10	7/22
5	4/11–5/11	8/12
6	5/12–6/10	9/9
7	6/11–7/12	10/8
8	7/13–8/10	10/29
9	8/11–9/10	1/13/88[a]
10	9/11–10/13	1/12/88[a]
11	10/14–11/10	2/11
12	11/12–12/10	2/19
1	12/11/87–1/11/88	3/24
2	1/12–2/10	4/15
3	2/11–3/10	5/13
4	3/11–4/11	6/22
5	4/12–5/10	8/5
6	5/11–6/10	8/18

[a] Delayed and transposed by the Crash.

learning about an insider transaction is normally about three and a half months. However, such a time delay does not nullify the value of *Official Summary*, because significant insider buying usually occurs more than four months in advance of favorable corporate news. In fact, to be deemed legally proper, an insider's purchase of the company's stock must be made well in advance of the disclosure of positive news or unexpected favorable developments. Furthermore, according to the Securities Exchange Act of 1934, an insider is not permitted to buy and sell the company's stock for a profit within a holding period of less than six months.

legal constraints on insider transactions

For purposes of screening the *Official Summary* to obtain useful data, one must define precisely what constitutes *significant insider buying* (abbreviated *sib*). A somewhat sharpened and updated version of the practical screening definition used by others[9] will be employed here: *sib* is said to appear in *Official Summary* if three or more insiders purchase their company's stock in the open market during a one-month reporting period, with no sale of the stock by any insider during the period, and the total market value of the insider purchases exceeds $100,000. By requiring three or more insiders to make purchases and none to make a sale, the *sib* definition reflects an insider consensus opinion regarding

sib

the value of the company's open market-priced stock.

---
sib examples

Reproduced on pages 30-85 are examples of *sib* by insiders of Avon Products (AVP), BankAmerica (BAC), Bell Atlantic (BEL), Kentucky Utilities (KU), Consolidated Stores (CNS), GAF Corporation (GAF), CalMat (CZM), Lomas & Nettleton Financial (LNF), BRT Realty Trust (BRT), Redman Industries (RE), Continental Illinois (CIL), Pier 1 Imports (PIR), Best Products (BES) and General Electric (GE) in Volumes 53 and 54 of the *Official Summary*. Also shown for purposes of comparison are some transactions by insiders of companies that appear alphabetized adjacent to the companies with *sib* entries. Open market purchases are signified by a "P" in the column marked "Character" for the transaction, while other symbols in the Character column (e.g.,

---
*character of
insider
transactions*

"B" for acquisition through a plan, "X" for acquisition by exercise of a stock option, "T" for other acquisition, etc.) label irrelevant purchase transactions [usually made at prices well below the then prevailing open market (NYSE) price asso-

Character of Transactions in *Official Summary*

"3"-	Initial statement of ownership
"B"-	Acquisition of shares accrued through a plan
"D"-	Stock dividend
"F"-	Exercise of rights, etc.
"G"-	Acquired by gift
"H"-	Disposed of by gift
"J"-	Private purchase
"K"-	Private sale
"M"-	Acquisition by exchange or conversion
"N"-	Disposed of by exchange or conversion
"P"-	Open market purchase
"Q"-	Disposition by exercise of option
"R"-	Redeemed *(Called, matured or retired)*
"S"-	Open market sale
"T"-	Other acquisition
"U"-	Other disposition
"V"-	Disposition of warrants by exercise
"W"-	Acquisition by exercise of warrants
"X"-	Acquisition by exercise of options
"Y"-	Reverse stock split
"Z"-	Stock split

ciated with "P" purchases]. The *Official Summary* table for the meaning of all Character symbols is reproduced above to elucidate the transaction data on the following pages.

(From No. 2 of Vol. 53, received by subscribers on or about May 21, 1987)

OFFICIAL SUMMARY OF

ISSUER
  SECURITY
    REPORTING PERSON
      NATURE OF OWNERSHIP
	Relationship	Date of trans-action	Character	Late, amended or inconsistent

AVON PRODS INC				
COM				
CHAMBERLIN JOHN S	O			
DIRECT		12/10/86	X	L
GAULT STANLEY C	D			
DIRECT		01/13/87	P	
MOSBACHER EMIL JR	D			
DIRECT		01/13/87	P	
PROCCPE ERNESTA G	D			
DIRECT		12/01/86	D	L
DIRECT		12/05/86	T	L
WALDRON HICKS B	D			
DIRECT		12/01/86	D	L
DIRECT		01/12/87	P	
INDIRECT		12/31/86	B	L
AZTECH INTL LTD				
COM				
SCHMITT HARRISON H	D			
DIRECT		12/24/86	J	A

SECURITY TRANSACTIONS AND HOLDINGS

TRANSACTIONS				Month end holdings of securities
Bought or otherwise acquired		Sold or otherwise disposed of		
Amount	Price	Amount	Price	
1,748	$21.06			5,048
500	$26.50			1,000
2,700	$26.50			1,000
41	$29.90			
165	$30.00			2,708
2,257				
3,000	$27.00			26,249
40	$27.00			1
2,000	$1.13			2,000

Total amount of Avon Products *sib* (open market "P" purchases) during period: $166,000.

(From No. 3 of Vol. 53, received by subscribers on or about June 19, 1987)

OFFICIAL SUMMARY OF				

ISSUER
  SECURITY
    REPORTING PERSON
      NATURE OF OWNERSHIP
	Relationship	Date of trans-action	Character	Late, amended or inconsistent

AVON PRODS INC				
COM				
HENN WILLIAM R	O			
DIRECT......................		01/14/87	P	L
KNIGHT WILLIAM THOMAS	O			
DIRECT......................		01/12/87	P	L
INDIRECT		12/31/85	B	L
INDIRECT		09/30/86	B	L
INDIRECT		12/31/86	B	L
PRESTON JAMES E	OD			
DIRECT......................		01/14/87	P	L
INDIRECT		01/31/87	B	L
STARRETT CAM	O			
DIRECT......................		01/13/87	X	L
WILLETT WILLIAM H	O			
DIRECT......................		01/31/87	B	L
INDIRECT		01/31/87	T	L
ZIMMERMAN JULES	O			
DIRECT......................		01/12/87	P	L
INDIRECT		01/31/87	B	L
AYDIN CORP				
COM				
MILLER B JACK	O			
DIRECT......................		01/06/87	X	L
INDIRECT		02/12/87		

SECURITY TRANSACTIONS AND HOLDINGS				
TRANSACTIONS				Month end holdings of securities
Bought or otherwise acquired		Sold or otherwise disposed of		
Amount	Price	Amount	Price	
1,000	$26.38			2,000
400	$26.88			930
67	$27.63			
12	$32.88			1
76				
1,500	$27.38			7,076
2,576				1,349
500	$25.70			500
1,000				1
304				1
1,000	$26.88			2,218
218				1
1,334	$17.39			1,434
				55

Total amount of Avon products *sib* (open market "P" purchases) during period: $105,000.

(From No. 4 of Vol. 53, received by subscribers on about July 22, 1987)

OFFICIAL SUMMARY OF

ISSUER
  SECURITY
    REPORTING PERSON
      NATURE OF OWNERSHIP
	Relationship	Date of trans-action	Character	Late, amended or inconsistent

DIRECT		02/03/87	S	L
BANK BLDG & EQUIP CORP AMER				
COM				
WEIS CARL J	O			
DIRECT		02/12/87	T	L
INDIRECT		03/25/87		
BANK DEL CORP				
COM				
SHEA JEREMIAH P	D			
DIRECT		03/06/87	X	
INDIRECT		04/08/87		
BANK NEW YORK INC				
COM				
MERRILL NEWTON P S	O			
DIRECT		02/02/87	P	L
DIRECT		02/06/87	D	L
INDIRECT		03/17/87		
BANK SOUTH CORP				
COM				
CARPER ROBERT A	O			
DIRECT		03/11/87		
INDIRECT		01/01/87	B	L
BANK VA CO				
COM				
BERWANGER ROGER H	AF			
DIRECT		02/18/87	S	L

SECURITY TRANSACTIONS AND HOLDINGS

| TRANSACTIONS | | | | Month end holdings of securities |
| Bought or otherwise acquired | | Sold or otherwise disposed of | | |
Amount	Price	Amount	Price	
		2,500	$21.88	680
395				12,981
				1,155
500	$18.30			8,000
				14,201
28	$38.10			
42	$37.58			5,911
				3,070
				3,575
220				1,891
		1,500	$33.75	5,696

(table continues)

OFFICIAL SUMMARY OF

ISSUER
  SECURITY
    REPORTING PERSON
      NATURE OF OWNERSHIP
	Relationship	Date of trans-action	Character	Late, amended or inconsistent

MOORE ANDREW TAYLOR JR	O			
DIRECT		03/31/87	B	
MYERS SARA REDDING	O			
DIRECT		02/27/87	B	L
TROUT KENNETH H	O			
DIRECT		02/27/87	B	L
DIRECT		03/09/87	X	
BANKEAST CORP				
COM				
DEWITT WALTER N	D			
DIRECT		03/13/87	X	
DIRECT		03/19/87	X	
INDIRECT		03/24/87		
BANKAMERICA CORP				
COM				
ASH ROY L	D			
DIRECT		03/25/87	P	
BECKETT JOHN RAYMOND	D			
DIRECT		03/27/87	P	
BRENNER BARBARA A	O			
DIRECT		03/16/87		
INDIRECT		12/31/86	B	L
COOPER THOMAS A	O			
DIRECT		10/12/86	3	A
INDIRECT		10/12/86	3	A
HAWLEY PHILIP M	D			
DIRECT		03/30/87	P	
MAIER CORNELL C	D			
DIRECT		03/23/87	P	

SECURITY TRANSACTIONS AND HOLDINGS

TRANSACTIONS				Month end holdings of securities
Bought or otherwise acquired		Sold or otherwise disposed of		
Amount	Price	Amount	Price	
23	$30.07			2,042
28	$31.88			276
31	$31.88			3,736
1,000	$26.06			4,736
9,000	$2.13			
22,320	$2.98			31,320
				3,894
6,463	$12.50			10,000
1,000	$12.38			26,000
				300
42	$14.22			221
				1,000
				25,734
600	$12.25			1,000
1,000	$12.50			1,500

Total amount of BankAmerica *sib* during period: $113,000.

(From No. 5 of Vol. 53, received by subscribers on or about August 12, 1987)

OFFICIAL SUMMARY OF

ISSUER
  SECURITY
    REPORTING PERSON
      NATURE OF OWNERSHIP
	Relationship	Date of trans-action	Character	Late, amended or inconsistent

COM				
HAUSMAN JACK	D			
DIRECT		04/09/87	P	
BELL & HOWELL CO				
COM				
DONALDSON W J	O			
DIRECT		03/05/87	S	L
BELL ATLANTIC CORP				
COM				
HALPIN GERALD T	D			
DIRECT		01/02/87	B	L
DIRECT		02/02/87	B	L
INDIRECT		05/08/87		
HARRISON ROBERT D	D			
DIRECT		04/24/87	P	
INDIRECT		05/08/87		
MAYPOLE JOHN F	D			
DIRECT		04/14/87	P	
INDIRECT		04/14/87	P	
YOUNG SHIRLEY	D			
DIRECT		01/02/87	B	L
DIRECT		02/01/87	B	L
DIRECT		02/02/87	B	L
DIRECT		04/02/87	P	
INDIRECT		05/08/87		
BELL INDS				
COM				
WILLIAMS THEODORE E	O			
DIRECT		04/30/87	S	
INDIRECT		05/01/87		

SECURITY TRANSACTIONS AND HOLDINGS

| TRANSACTIONS | | | | Month end holdings of securities |
| Bought or otherwise acquired | | Sold or otherwise disposed of | | |
Amount	Price	Amount	Price	
1,500	$23.00			66,692
		2,200	$43.50	200
106	$69.38			
35	$69.38			3,400
				241
200	$64.00			1,038
				8
500	$62.00			1,560
500	$62.75			2,784
94	$69.38			
6	$74.29			
23	$69.38			
1,000	$66.50			2,115
				400
		5,000	$24.63	202,500
				2,200

(Tables continues)

OFFICIAL SUMMARY OF

ISSUER
  SECURITY
    REPORTING PERSON
      NATURE OF OWNERSHIP
	Relationship	Date of trans-action	Character	Late, amended or inconsistent

BELMONT BANCORP				
COM				
FOGT MARK S	D			
DIRECT		05/06/87		
INDIRECT		04/27/87	J	
BELO A H CORP				
COM				
OSBORNE BURL	AF			
DIRECT		12/19/86	3	A
INDIRECT		12/19/86	3	A
SHEEHAN JAMES P	O			
DIRECT		12/19/86	B	A
BENEFICIAL CORP				
COM				
CASPERSEN FINN M W	D			
DIRECT		03/01/87	B	A
INDIRECT		03/01/87	D	A
STEPHENSON ANN	AF			
DIRECT		06/28/85	T	L
DIRECT		02/27/87	B	L
DIRECT		03/04/87	U	L
DIRECT		03/31/87	B	L
TUCKER ROBERT A	D			
DIRECT		03/06/87	S	L
INDIRECT		03/06/87	S	L
INDIRECT		03/09/87	S	L

SECURITY TRANSACTIONS AND HOLDINGS

| TRANSACTIONS | | | | Month end holdings of securities |
| Bought or otherwise acquired | | Sold or otherwise disposed of | | |
Amount	Price	Amount	Price	
85	$23.00			557 175
7,500				7,208 61 11,550
2,205	$62.75			50,992
12	$39.07			721,715
10				
387	$59.25			
		1,203	$64.50	
447	$62.75			844
		6,000	$62.05	35,000
		7,852	$62.05	
		70	$60.63	12,150

Total amount of Bell Atlantic *sib* (open market "P" purchases) during period: $142,000.

(From No. 5 of Vol. 53, received by subscribers on or about August 12, 1987)

OFFICIAL SUMMARY OF

ISSUER
  SECURITY
    REPORTING PERSON
      NATURE OF OWNERSHIP
	Relationship	Date of trans-action	Character	Late, amended or inconsistent

KENTUCKY UTILS CO				
COM				
DUKE ANDREW C	D			
DIRECT		04/29/87	P	
INDIRECT		05/04/87		
HEWETT ROBERT M	O			
DIRECT		04/13/87	P	
INDIRECT		04/13/87	P	
HILLENMEYER WALTER W JR	D			
DIRECT		04/29/87		
INDIRECT		04/10/87	P	
NEWTON JOHN T	O			
DIRECT		04/03/87	P	
INDIRECT		05/06/87		
ROSENTHAL WARREN W	D			
DIRECT		04/23/87	P	
KEUFFEL & ESSER CO				
COM				
LAWHON RAYMOND C	OD			
DIRECT		04/09/87	S	
MILLER JOHN P	D			
DIRECT		04/09/87	U	
KEYCORP				
COM				
CARLSON CURTIS M	O			
DIRECT		03/23/87	X	L

SECURITY TRANSACTIONS AND HOLDINGS				
TRANSACTIONS				Month end holdings of securities
Bought or otherwise acquired		Sold or otherwise disposed of		
Amount	Price	Amount	Price	
1,700	$37.63			2,200
				200
54	$34.75			54
54	$34.75			1,364
				2,400
1,000	$34.00			2,200
200	$37.13			1,096
				4,239
1,000	$36.50			1,200
		2,000	$1.00	
		1,000	$1.00	
3,750	$12.67			6,888

(table continues)

OFFICIAL SUMMARY OF

ISSUER
  SECURITY
    REPORTING PERSON
      NATURE OF OWNERSHIP
	Relationship	Date of trans-action	Character	Late, amended or inconsistent

ESPE ARNOLD G	OD			
DIRECT		04/27/87	S	
WARD F JAY	O			
DIRECT		03/23/87	X	L
KEYSTONE CONS INDS INC				
COM				
OWENS NICHOLAS R	O			
DIRECT		04/27/87		
INDIRECT		03/10/87	U	A
INDIRECT		03/31/87	B	L
KEYSTONE INTL INC				
COM				
LEBLANC RAYMOND ALBERT	OD			
DIRECT		03/03/87	S	L
DIRECT		03/06/87	S	L
INDIRECT		03/01/87	D	L
KIMBERLY CLARK CORP				
COM				
KIMB. CLARK SALARIED EMP.	AF			
DIRECT		04/01/87	U	
DIRECT		04/28/87	U	
KING INTL CORP				
COM				
KASSNER FRED	D			
DIRECT		03/20/87	T	L
DIRECT		03/26/87	T	L
INDIRECT		04/16/87		

SECURITY TRANSACTIONS AND HOLDINGS

TRANSACTIONS				Month end holdings of securities
Bought or otherwise acquired		Sold or otherwise disposed of		
Amount	Price	Amount	Price	
		1,000	$26.75	27,650
1,440	$12.67			5,005
		225	$10.38	17,700 4,593
212				4,804
		4,000 12,000	$19.00 $19.00	139,090
10	$19.00			18,807
		1,962 1,704		2,247,190
1,000	$9.00			
100	$9.00			669,542 53,700

Total amount of Kentucky Utilities *sib* during period: $146,000.

(From No. 7 of Vol. 53, received by subscribers on or about October 8, 1987)

OFFICIAL SUMMARY OF

ISSUER
  SECURITY
    REPORTING PERSON
      NATURE OF OWNERSHIP
	Relationship	Date of trans-action	Character	Late, amended or inconsistent

CONSOLIDATED STORES CORP				
COM				
KING PATRICIA L	O			
DIRECT		01/02/87	P	L
DIRECT		05/04/87	P	L
SHENK CHARLES H	H			
INDIRECT		05/04/87	P	L
INDIRECT		05/14/87	P	L
INDIRECT		05/18/87	P	A
SHENK SOL A	H			
DIRECT		05/04/87	P	L
DIRECT		05/04/87	P	A
DIRECT		05/14/87	P	A
DIRECT		05/14/87	P	A
INDIRECT		05/04/87	P	L
INDIRECT		05/04/87	P	A
INDIRECT		05/14/87	P	L
INDIRECT		05/14/87	P	A

SECURITY TRANSACTIONS AND HOLDINGS				
TRANSACTIONS				Month end holdings of securities
Bought or otherwise acquired		Sold or otherwise disposed of		
Amount	Price	Amount	Price	
200	$14.50			200
500	$10.00			700
150,000	$9.63			
71,000	$9.38			6,694,152
2,500	$9.50			6,711,652
25,000	$9.38			
25,000	$9.38			
6,000	$9.50			
34,000	$9.38			45,000
125,000	$9.63			
25,000	$9.63			
71,000	$9.38			6,694,152
2,500	$9.50			6,711,652

(table continues)

OFFICIAL SUMMARY OF

ISSUER SECURITY REPORTING PERSON NATURE OF OWNERSHIP	Relationship	Date of trans-action	Character	Late, amended or inconsistent
CONSUMER PLASTICS CORP				
COM				
RYAN MICHAEL G	D			
DIRECT		06/30/87	P	A
CONSUMERS FINL CORP				
COM				
COOLING WALTER R	D			
DIRECT		03/25/86	T	L
GRONINGER JOHN E	D			
DIRECT		12/04/84	T	L
DIRECT		05/20/86	P	L
DIRECT		06/04/86	P	L
DIRECT		06/04/86	T	L
LITTLE ROBERT G JR	D			
DIRECT		07/08/86	T	L
CONSUMERS PWR CO				
PFD $4.50				
MIRABITO PAUL S	D			
DIRECT		05/04/87	T	A

SECURITY TRANSACTIONS AND HOLDINGS

TRANSACTIONS				Month end holdings of securities
Bought or otherwise acquired		Sold or otherwise disposed of		
Amount	Price	Amount	Price	
2,000	$11.50			2,000
4,491	$6.00			34,540
102	$3.00			
1,000	$4.63			
1,000	$4.63			
182	$4.00			24,137
100	$4.69			8,900
10	$46.60			10

Total amount of Consolidated Stores *sib* during period: $2,987,000.

(From No. 7 of Vol. 53, received by subscribers on or about October 8, 1987)

OFFICIAL SUMMARY OF

ISSUER
  SECURITY
    REPORTING PERSON
      NATURE OF OWNERSHIP
	Relationship	Date of trans-action	Character	Late, amended or inconsistent

BARTELS JOHN F	O			
DIRECT		03/09/87	X	L
DIRECT		03/09/87	U	L
INDIRECT		06/16/87		
BROWN COLIN W	O			
DIRECT		05/26/87	X	L
INDIRECT		06/18/87		
DODGE WILLIAM D	O			
DIRECT		06/12/87	X	
DIRECT		06/12/87	U	
INDIRECT		07/08/87		
MALIZIA A A..	D			
DIRECT		05/29/87	X	L
DIRECT		05/29/87	U	L
INDIRECT		06/18/87		
FUR VAULT INC				
COM				
SOLOMON MICHAEL	D			
DIRECT		06/18/87		
INDIRECT		05/18/87	P	L
INDIRECT		05/20/87	P	L
FUTURA WEST INC				
COM				
QUAID WILLIAM J	O			
DIRECT		05/18/87	J	L

SECURITY TRANSACTIONS AND HOLDINGS

TRANSACTIONS				Month end holdings of securities
Bought or otherwise acquired		Sold or otherwise disposed of		
Amount	Price	Amount	Price	
2,500				
		1,435		20,514
				5,243
2,000				8,870
				660
750				
		200		8,310
				6,279
5,075				
		2,531		43,118
				5,300
				40,000
3,700	$7.88			
1,000	$7.75			4,700
200	$1.50			21,300

(table continues)

OFFICIAL SUMMARY OF

ISSUER
  SECURITY
    REPORTING PERSON
      NATURE OF OWNERSHIP
	Relationship	Date of trans-action	Character	Late, amended or inconsistent

GAF CORP				
COM				
CARROLL DANIEL T	D			
DIRECT		05/26/87	P	
DIRECT		06/09/87	P	
GOLDMAN JACOB E	D			
DIRECT		05/20/87	P	L
LYONS WILLIAM P	D			
DIRECT		05/20/87	P	L
INDIRECT		06/22/87		
ROGERS SCOTT A JR	D			
DIRECT		05/20/87	P	L
DIRECT		06/03/87	P	
DIRECT		06/10/87	P	
TYDINGS JOSEPH C	D			
DIRECT		05/26/87	P	L
DIRECT		06/05/87	H	
DIRECT		06/10/87	P	
INDIRECT		07/10/87		
GCA CORPORATION				
COM				
BRUNING JOHN R	OD			
DIRECT		04/23/87	T	A
DIRECT		05/21/87	U	
INDIRECT		06/12/87		

SECURITY TRANSACTIONS AND HOLDINGS

TRANSACTIONS				Month end holdings of securities
Bought or otherwise acquired		Sold or otherwise disposed of		
Amount	Price	Amount	Price	
262	$47.50			2,262
249	$50.29			2,511
364	$45.75			7,030
5,730	$45.75			5,730
				54,000
545	$45.75			2,545
508	$49.25			
496	$50.38			3,549
262	$47.50			2,116
		150		
248	$50.38			2,214
				5,100
8,800				4,411
		35		4,411
				1,766

Total amount of GAF Corporation *sib* during period: $398,000.

(From No. 8 of Vol. 53, received by subscribers on or about October 29, 1987)

OFFICIAL SUMMARY OF

ISSUER
  SECURITY
    REPORTING PERSON
      NATURE OF OWNERSHIP
	Relationship	Date of trans-action	Character	Late, amended or inconsistent

CAESARS WORLD INC COM				
LANNI J TERRENCE	D			
DIRECT		07/10/87	S	
YELLEN MANUEL	D			
DIRECT		07/29/87	S	
CALGON CARBON CORP COM				
WEIL HARRY H	D			
INDIRECT		07/07/87	P	A
CALIFORNIA MICROWAVE INC COM				
HERSHBERG DAVID E	O			
DIRECT		07/09/87	B	
CALLAHAN MNG CORP COM				
METTHAM JOHN T	O			
DIRECT		07/01/87	S	
INDIRECT		07/28/87		

SECURITY TRANSACTIONS AND HOLDINGS

TRANSACTIONS				Month end holdings of securities
Bought or otherwise acquired		Sold or otherwise disposed of		
Amount	Price	Amount	Price	
		44,617	$34.63	20,625
		10,000	$34.63	2,210
750	$31.00			750
537	$6.38			50,355
		200	$27.50	2,432
				1

(table continues)

| | OFFICIAL SUMMARY OF | | | |

ISSUER
  SECURITY
    REPORTING PERSON
      NATURE OF OWNERSHIP
	Relationship	Date of trans-action	Character	Late, amended or inconsistent

CALMAT CO				
COM				
HICKS ALBERT J	D			
DIRECT		05/07/87	P	L
INDIRECT		05/07/87	P	L
INDIRECT		05/07/87	P	L
HUSTON WILLIAM T	D			
DIRECT		07/21/87	P	
INDIRECT		08/05/87		
INDUSTRIAL EQUITY LTD	B			
INDIRECT		07/27/87	P	
INDIRECT		07/28/87	P	
INDIRECT		07/29/87	P	
INDIRECT		07/30/87	P	
CAMBRIDGE BIOSCIENCE CORP				
COM				
RAYNOVICH ROD N	O			
DIRECT		06/24/87	T	L
DIRECT		07/10/87	U	
CAMBRIDGE MED TECH. CORP				
COM				
BONANNO FRANK C	O			
DIRECT		06/30/87	3	
CAMPBELL RES INC				
COM				
LISTER RICHARD L	O			
DIRECT		06/30/87	B	L

SECURITY TRANSACTIONS AND HOLDINGS

TRANSACTIONS				Month end holdings of securities
Bought or otherwise acquired		Sold or otherwise disposed of		
Amount	Price	Amount	Price	
1,000	$33.50			9,054
4,000	$34.13			1
1,000	$33.50			
1,000	$30.50			4,140
				3,600
1,400	$27.99			
28,600	$28.10			
14,700	$28.11			
300,000	$29.50			4,493,470
4,000	$10.25			
		4,000	$10.25	1,918
				33,115
2,396	$3.13			81,621

Total amount of CalMat *sib* during period: $10,300,000.

(From No. 11 of Vol. 53, received by subscribers on or about February 1, 1988)

OFFICIAL SUMMARY OF

ISSUER
  SECURITY
    REPORTING PERSON
      NATURE OF OWNERSHIP
	Relationship	Date of trans-action	Character	Late, amended or inconsistent

LOCKHEED CORP				
P				
COM				
BARNARD LOUIS JOSEPH	D			
DIRECT		10/02/87	X	
VAN SCHAICK ANTHONY G	O			
DIRECT		10/27/87	S	
LODGISTIX INC				
COM				
LEW JAMES W	OD			
DIRECT		10/28/87	T	
DIRECT		10/28/87	T	
DIRECT		10/29/87	T	
DIRECT		10/30/87	T	
LOGICON INC				
COM				
DALTON JAMES E	AF			
DIRECT		10/26/87	P	
DICKERMAN ROBERT S	D			
DIRECT		10/26/87	P	A
DIRECT		10/27/87	P	A
DIRECT		10/30/87	P	A

SECURITY TRANSACTIONS AND HOLDINGS

TRANSACTIONS				Month end holdings of securities
Bought or otherwise acquired		Sold or otherwise disposed of		
Amount	Price	Amount	Price	
2,700	$34.81			2,700
		3,000	$36.13	
1,000	$2.00			
1,000	$2.13			
1,600	$2.13			
1,000	$2.06			135,601
1,000	$15.75			11,000
1,000	$21.88			
1,000	$18.25			
1,000	$16.00			6,000

(table continues)

OFFICIAL SUMMARY OF

ISSUER
  SECURITY
    REPORTING PERSON
      NATURE OF OWNERSHIP
	Relationship	Date of trans-action	Character	Late, amended or inconsistent

LOMAS & NETTLETON FINL CORP				
COM				
ENLOE ROBERT TED	O			
DIRECT		09/30/87	P	L
HAY JESS THOMAS	D			
DIRECT		09/24/87	P	L
DIRECT		09/25/87	P	L
DIRECT		09/30/87	P	L
INDIRECT		10/13/87		
KELLY DAVID JR	O			
DIRECT		09/30/87	P	L
SEXTON JOHN F	O			
DIRECT		09/23/87	P	L
DIRECT		10/12/87	X	
STEPHENS DAVID C	O			
DIRECT		09/30/87	P	L
TAYLOR RAMONA	D			
DIRECT		09/30/87	P	L
INDIRECT		10/15/87		
WHITE GARY M	O			
DIRECT		09/30/87	P	L
WOOTEN JAMES M	D			
DIRECT		09/30/87	P	L

SECURITY TRANSACTIONS AND HOLDINGS

| TRANSACTIONS | | | | Month end holdings of securities |
| Bought or otherwise acquired | | Sold or otherwise disposed of | | |
Amount	Price	Amount	Price	
37,500	$24.88			169,763
27,400	$23.88			
121,600	$25.08			
1,000	$24.99			401,112
				377,408
5,000	$24.88			46,247
50,000	$23.88			160,594
15,000	$21.66			175,594
4,000	$24.88			4,000
3,000	$24.88			16,358
				10,000
4,000	$24.88			8,500
10,000	$24.88			101,480

Total amount of Lomas & Nettleton Financial *sib* during period: $6,700,000.

(From No. 12 of Vol. 53, received by subscribers on or about February 19, 1988)

OFFICIAL SUMMARY OF

ISSUER
  SECURITY
    REPORTING PERSON
      NATURE OF OWNERSHIP
	Relationship	Date of trans-action	Character	Late, amended or inconsistent

REGAZZI JOHN H	O			
DIRECT		10/26/87	P	
AVON PRODS INC				
COM				
BLOCK RUTH S	D			
DIRECT		10/20/87	P	
WALDRON HICKS B	D			
DIRECT		08/19/87	T	L
DIRECT		10/20/87	T	L
INDIRECT		11/16/87		
AZTECH INTL LTD				
COM				
GROUNDS LOUIS N	O			
DIRECT		11/24/87	3	
BEI HLDGS LTD				
COM				
TERRELL ELLEN T MS	O			
DIRECT		07/01/87	3	
WALLACE RONALD D	O			
DIRECT		03/12/87	3	
BRT RLTY TR				
SH BEN INT				
CARVER EUGENE P	D			
DIRECT		05/21/87	P	L
INDIRECT		04/21/87	T	L
INDIRECT		11/05/87	P	

SECURITY TRANSACTIONS AND HOLDINGS

TRANSACTIONS				Month end holdings of securities
Bought or otherwise acquired		Sold or otherwise disposed of		
Amount	Price	Amount	Price	
1,000	$18.50			18,550
200	$23.50			400
2,492 2,000	$22.00			32,068 1
				5,000
				7,000
				77,000
200	$29.88			10,000
11,571 4,000	$24.25			17,221

(table continues)

OFFICIAL SUMMARY OF

ISSUER
  SECURITY
    REPORTING PERSON
      NATURE OF OWNERSHIP
	Relationship	Date of trans-action	Character	Late, amended or inconsistent

GOULD FREDRIC	D			
DIRECT		11/16/87		
INDIRECT		10/19/87	P	L
INDIRECT		10/21/87	P	L
INDIRECT		10/22/87	P	L
INDIRECT		10/27/87	P	L
GOULD MATTHEW J	O			
DIRECT		11/16/87		
INDIRECT		10/22/87	P	L
GOULD STUART S	AF			
DIRECT		11/16/87		
INDIRECT		10/21/87	P	L
INDIRECT		10/22/87	P	L
INDIRECT		10/27/87	P	L
KEELY EUGENE J	O			
DIRECT		11/16/87		
INDIRECT		10/19/87	P	L
KUPIN NATHAN	O			
DIRECT		11/16/87		
INDIRECT		10/21/87	P	L
INDIRECT		10/22/87	P	L
INDIRECT		10/27/87	P	L
ROSENZWEIG ISRAEL	O			
DIRECT		11/16/87		
INDIRECT		10/19/87	P	L

SECURITY TRANSACTIONS AND HOLDINGS

TRANSACTIONS				Month end holdings of securities
Bought or otherwise acquired		Sold or otherwise disposed of		
Amount	Price	Amount	Price	
				124,415
2,000	$15.75			
5,000	$16.63			
6,129	$16.00			
2,500	$15.88			431,810
				23,597
2,500	$16.00			3,235
				63,155
5,000	$16.63			
3,629	$16.00			
2,500	$15.88			289,164
				6,833
2,000	$15.75			10,300
				45,499
5,000	$16.63			
3,629	$16.00			
2,500	$15.88			253,596
				84,269
2,000	$15.75			10,925

Total amount of BRT Realty Trust *sib* during period: $1,380,000.

(From No. 1 of Vol. 54, received by subscribers on or about March 24, 1988)

OFFICIAL SUMMARY OF

ISSUER
  SECURITY
    REPORTING PERSON
      NATURE OF OWNERSHIP
	Relationship	Date of trans- action	Character	Late, amended or inconsistent

REDMAN INDS INC				
COM				
BABB FRED	O			
DIRECT		12/01/87	P	
DIRECT		12/04/87	P	
GUERIN DEAN P	D			
DIRECT		11/24/87	P	L
DIRECT		12/02/87	P	
REDMAN JAMES	D			
DIRECT		11/17/87	P	L
DIRECT		11/18/87	P	L
INDIRECT		12/15/87		
REFLECTONE INC				
COM				
BETTKE EDWARD W	D			
DIRECT		11/17/87	P	L
REGIS CORP				
COM				
KUNIN MYRON	H			
DIRECT		12/14/87		
INDIRECT		11/12/87	S	L
REPUBLIC BANCORP INC				
COM				
SMITH GEORGE B	D			
DIRECT		12/14/87	3	

SECURITY TRANSACTIONS AND HOLDINGS

TRANSACTIONS				Month end holdings of securities
Bought or otherwise acquired		Sold or otherwise disposed of		
Amount	Price	Amount	Price	
1,000	$6.00			
1,000	$5.75			1
1,200	$6.00			6,200
800	$6.00			7,000
150,000	$6.25			
55,600	$6.09			526,280
				1,063,272
450	$9.95			1,000
				6,656,000
		15,000	$11.50	5,926,000
				166,975

(table continues)

OFFICIAL SUMMARY OF

ISSUER
  SECURITY
    REPORTING PERSON
      NATURE OF OWNERSHIP
	Relationship	Date of trans-action	Character	Late, amended or inconsistent

REPUBLIC GYPSUM CO				
COM				
GREEN W TOM	D			
DIRECT		12/21/87		
INDIRECT		11/02/87	P	L
INDIRECT		11/27/87	P	L
REPUBLIC N Y CORP				
COM				
SAFRA EDMOND J	B			
INDIRECT		11/02/87	P	
INDIRECT		11/04/87	P	
INDIRECT		11/05/87	P	
INDIRECT		11/10/87	P	
INDIRECT		11/12/87	P	
RESEARCH INC				
COM				
SANGSTER GORDON W	AF			
DIRECT		11/10/87	B	L
WILSON KENNETH C	O			
DIRECT		10/28/87	P	L
INDIRECT		10/28/87	P	L

SECURITY TRANSACTIONS AND HOLDINGS

| TRANSACTIONS | | | | Month end holdings of securities |
| Bought or otherwise acquired | | Sold or otherwise disposed of | | |
Amount	Price	Amount	Price	
				132,644
1,400	$5.38			
600	$5.38			66,858
3,200	$41.50			
2,500	$40.00			
2,500	$39.75			
10,000	$38.50			
4,500	$39.00			9,750,760
49				6,549
1,000	$9.50			1,000
250	$9.50			250

Total amount of Redman Industries *sib* during period: $1,300,000.

(From No. 1 of Vol. 54, received by subscribers on or about March 24, 1988)

OFFICIAL SUMMARY OF

ISSUER SECURITY REPORTING PERSON NATURE OF OWNERSHIP	Relationship	Date of trans-action	Character	Late, amended or inconsistent
CONSTELLATION BANCORP COM STEGEL JOEL D DIRECT	AF	11/14/87	B	L
CONTEL CORP COM SLOAN HOWARD DIRECT .... INDIRECT	D	12/30/87 01/05/88	P	
CONTINENTAL CORP COM ZIPF GEORGE G DIRECT	D	10/30/87	P	L
CONTINENTAL GEN INS CO COM KAMPE LESTER C DIRECT .... INDIRECT	O	12/08/87 01/06/88	X	
CONTINENTAL ILL CORP COM P BOTTUM EDWARD S	AF			

SECURITY TRANSACTIONS AND HOLDINGS

| TRANSACTIONS | | | | Month end holdings of securities |
| Bought or otherwise acquired | | Sold or otherwise disposed of | | |
Amount	Price	Amount	Price	
40	$25.18			7,495
2,400	$28.25			16,851 6,751
500	$37.50			3,000
363	$2.27			12,922 27

(table continues)

OFFICIAL SUMMARY OF

ISSUER
  SECURITY
    REPORTING PERSON
      NATURE OF OWNERSHIP
	Relationship	Date of trans-action	Character	Late, amended or inconsistent

DIRECT		11/05/87	P	L
INDIRECT		12/14/87		
HUMAN PAUL M	O			
DIRECT		11/10/87	P	L
INDIRECT		12/14/87		
SWEARINGEN JOHN E	OD			
DIRECT		11/10/87	P	L
DIRECT		11/11/87	P	L
DIRECT		11/12/87	P	L
DIRECT		11/20/87	P	L
INDIRECT		12/14/87		
CONTINENTAL INFORMATION SYS CORP				
COM				
BIELING ALVIN O	AF			
DIRECT		12/06/87	T	A
DIRECT		12/07/87	T	A
DIRECT		12/08/87	T	A
PRINZING THOMAS	O			
DIRECT		11/10/87	X	L
INDIRECT		12/15/87		

SECURITY TRANSACTIONS AND HOLDINGS

TRANSACTIONS				Month end holdings of securities
Bought or otherwise acquired		Sold or otherwise disposed of		
Amount	Price	Amount	Price	
2,000	$3.13			3,000
				1,113
10,000	$3.00			10,000
				212
19,000	$3.00			
66,600	$3.00			
14,400	$3.00			
100,000	$2.75			208,600
				11,039
300	$5.63			
300	$5.63			
1,000	$5.38			6,440
9,000	$2.68			9,000
				82

Total amount of Continental Illinois *sib* during period: $1,620,000.

(From No. 2 of Vol. 54, received by subscribers on or about April 15, 1988)

OFFICIAL SUMMARY OF

ISSUER
  SECURITY
    REPORTING PERSON
      NATURE OF OWNERSHIP
	Relationship	Date of trans-action	Character	Late, amended or inconsistent

PIER 1 INC				
P				
COM				
CHRISTOPHER THOMAS A	AF			
DIRECT		01/08/88	P	
DIRECT		01/10/88	B	
DIRECT		01/11/88	P	
DIRECT		01/12/88	P	
DIRECT		01/13/88	P	
DIRECT		01/14/88	P	
DIRECT		01/15/88	P	
DIRECT		01/18/88	P	
DIRECT		01/19/88	P	
DIRECT		01/20/88	P	
DIRECT		01/21/88	P	
DIRECT		01/22/88	P	
INDIRECT		02/10/88		
GIROUARD MARVIN	AF			
DIRECT		01/08/88	P	
DIRECT		01/10/88	B	
DIRECT		01/11/88	P	
DIRECT		01/12/88	P	
DIRECT		01/13/88	P	
DIRECT		01/14/88	P	
DIRECT		01/15/88	P	
DIRECT		01/18/88	P	
DIRECT		01/19/88	P	
DIRECT`		`01/20/88	P	
DIRECT		01/21/88	P	
DIRECT		01/22/88	P	
JOHNSON CLARK A	O			
DIRECT		01/08/88	P	
DIRECT		01/10/88	B	
DIRECT		01/11/88	P	
DIRECT		01/12/88	P	
DIRECT		01/13/88	P	
DIRECT		01/14/88	P	
DIRECT		01/15/88	P	
DIRECT		01/18/88	P	
DIRECT		01/19/88	P	

SECURITY TRANSACTIONS AND HOLDINGS

TRANSACTIONS				Month end holdings of securities
Bought or otherwise acquired		Sold or otherwise disposed of		
Amount	Price	Amount	Price	
3,488	$6.38			
1,002	$7.31			
17,512	$6.13			
7,460	$5.88			
578	$5.88			
23,098	$5.75			
3,152	$5.88			
4,980	$5.88			
11,694	$5.88			
17,978	$6.00			
7,236	$6.00			
1,361	$6.00			153,335
				10,738
3,488	$6.38			
1,002	$7.31			
17,512	$6.13			
7,460	$5.88			
578	$5.88			
23,098	$5.75			
3,152	$5.88			
4,980	$5.88			
11,694	$5.88			
17,978	$6.00			
7,236	$6.00			
1,361	$6.00			182,646
6,978	$6.38			
1,519	$7.31			
35,044	$6.13			
14,928	$5.88			
1,157	$5.88			
46,221	$5.75			
6,307	$5.88			
9,964	$5.88			
23,399	$5.88			

(table continues)

OFFICIAL SUMMARY OF

ISSUER
  SECURITY
    REPORTING PERSON
      NATURE OF OWNERSHIP
	Relationship	Date of trans-action	Character	Late, amended or inconsistent

DIRECT		01/20/88	P	
DIRECT		01/21/88	P	
DIRECT		01/22/88	P	
KLAMON LAWRENCE P	D			
DIRECT		01/10/88	B	
MCKENZIE SALLY F MS	D			
DIRECT		12/02/87	P	L
DIRECT		12/25/87	H	L
DIRECT		01/10/88	B	
INDIRECT		02/10/88		
SCOTT CHARLES R	D			
DIRECT		01/10/88	B	
WARNER THOMAS N	D			
DIRECT		01/10/88	B	
INDIRECT		01/10/88		
WEATHERLY B MITCHELL	AF			
DIRECT		01/08/88	P	
DIRECT		01/10/88	B	
DIRECT		01/11/88	P	
DIRECT		01/12/88	P	
DIRECT		01/13/88	P	
DIRECT		01/14/88	P	
DIRECT		01/15/88	P	
DIRECT		01/18/88	P	
DIRECT		01/19/88	P	
DIRECT		01/20/88	P	
DIRECT		01/21/88	P	
DIRECT		01/22/88	P	
INDIRECT		01/31/88	H	
PIEZO ELEC PRODS INC				
COM				
BATES DONALD S	D			
DIRECT		11/23/87	3	
WTS				
ZANGARA ROBERT C	C			
DIRECT		01/15/87	3	

SECURITY TRANSACTIONS AND HOLDINGS

TRANSACTIONS				Month end holdings of securities
Bought or otherwise acquired		Sold or otherwise disposed of		
Amount	Price	Amount	Price	
35,975	$6.00			
14,480	$6.00			
2,724	$6.00			241,654
1,067	$7.31			14,169
60	$5.88			
		60		881
123	$7.31			1,004
				650
1,724	$7.31			11,387
1,066	$7.31			38,131
				519
699	$6.38			
497	$7.31			
3,512	$6.13			
1,496	$5.88			
116	$5.88			
4,632	$5.75			
632	$5.88			
998	$5.88			
2,345	$5.88			
3,605	$6.00			
1,452	$6.00			
274	$6.00			23,950
		200		1
				40,000
				300,000

Total amount of Pier 1 Imports *sib* during period: $2,500,000.

(From No. 5 of Vol. 54, received by subscribers on or about August 5, 1988)

OFFICIAL SUMMARY OF

ISSUER
  SECURITY
    REPORTING PERSON
      NATURE OF OWNERSHIP
	Relationship	Date of trans-action	Character	Late, amended or inconsistent

DOMBROWSKI LEON C	AF			
DIRECT		05/02/88	U	A
DIRECT		05/02/88	X	A
BEST BUY INC				
COM				
ZANATTA RANDALL R	O			
DIRECT		03/18/88	S	L
BEST PRODS INC				
COM				
BEASLEY P MARVIN	O			
DIRECT		03/31/88	P	L
COSTELLO WILLIAM F	O			
DIRECT		03/31/88	P	L
COTTINGHAM CHARLES G	O			
DIRECT		03/31/88	P	L
FLEMING E WOODROW	O			
DIRECT		03/30/88	X	L
GINSBERG MYRON P	O			
DIRECT		03/31/88	P	L
HAWKS J LEE	O			
DIRECT		03/30/88	X	L
HUNTLEY ROBERT E R	D			
DIRECT		03/31/88	P	L
KENDIG ROBERT A	C			
DIRECT		03/30/88	X	L
LEWIS FRANCES A	CD			
DIRECT		03/31/88	P	L
INDIRECT		03/29/88	U	
INDIRECT		03/31/88	P	L

SECURITY TRANSACTIONS AND HOLDINGS

TRANSACTIONS				Month end holdings of securities
Bought or otherwise acquired		Sold or otherwise disposed of		
Amount	Price	Amount	Price	
		6,667	$0.75	
50,000	$0.10			93,333
		5,500	$9.13	5,072
1,000	$11.88			1,000
7,073	$11.88			15,073
1,000	$11.88			1,000
3,789	$9.69			3,789
3,115	$11.88			3,115
6,231	$9.69			6,549
13,684	$11.88			20,721
5,894	$9.69			5,894
3,100	$11.88			258,557
15,000	$11.88	61,076		191,488

(table continues)

OFFICIAL SUMMARY OF

ISSUER
  SECURITY
    REPORTING PERSON
      NATURE OF OWNERSHIP
	Relationship	Date of trans-action	Character	Late, amended or inconsistent

LEWIS SYDNEY	CD			
DIRECT		03/31/88	P	L
INDIRECT		03/31/88	P	L
MAXWELL HENRY L	O			
DIRECT		03/30/88	X	L
PILLHISER ROSS R	D			
DIRECT		05/10/88		
INDIRECT		04/15/88	P	
MURPHY MARK M	O			
DIRECT		03/31/88	P	L
PARKER DUDLEY L JR	O			
DIRECT		03/31/88	P	L
PENN JOHN	O			
DIRECT		03/30/88	X	L
RILEY RICHARD T	O			
DIRECT		03/30/88	X	L
RUBIN DANIEL J	O			
DIRECT		03/30/88	X	L
INDIRECT		04/13/88		
SCHUNK THOMAS M	O			
DIRECT		03/30/88	X	L
SEITZINGER GEORGE	O			
DIRECT		03/30/88	X	L
SPENCER JAMES J	O			
DIRECT		03/31/88	P	L
INDIRECT		04/13/88		
STAUCCHAR JAMES C	O			
DIRECT		03/30/88	X	L
TENNENT WAYNE T	O			
DIRECT		03/30/88	X	L
WOLLENBERG FRED A	O			
DIRECT		03/30/88	X	L

SECURITY TRANSACTIONS AND HOLDINGS

TRANSACTIONS				Month end holdings of securities
Bought or otherwise acquired		Sold or otherwise disposed of		
Amount	Price	Amount	Price	
15,000	$11.88			191,488
3,100	$11.88			258,557
2,000	$9.69			2,400
				1,500
13,000	$11.00			18,000
1,250	$11.88			2,250
3,000	$11.88			3,000
2,947	$9.69			2,947
1,000	$9.69			1,000
2,000	$9.69			2,000
				300
2,000	$9.69			2,000
2,000	$9.69			2,425
3,400	$11.88			3,781
				1,350
2,000	$9.69			2,227
1,789	$9.69			2,464
4,200	$9.69			5,164

Total amount of Best Products *sib* during period (open market "P" purchases): $971,000.

(From No. 5 of Vol. 54, received by subscribers on or about August 5, 1988)

OFFICIAL SUMMARY OF

ISSUER
  SECURITY
    REPORTING PERSON
      NATURE OF OWNERSHIP
	Relationship	Date of trans-action	Character	Late, amended or inconsistent

DIRECT		03/07/88	S	L
DIRECT		03/16/88	S	L
MEYER RUSSELL W JR	OD			
DIRECT		03/01/88	T	
TRUXELL ROBERT W	O			
DIRECT		03/01/88	B	
DIRECT		03/16/88	S	
DIRECT		04/08/88	S	
GENERAL ELEC CO				
COM				
BOSSIDY LAWRENCE ARTHUR	D			
DIRECT		04/13/88	P	
INDIRECT		04/21/88		
PREISKEL BARBARA S MS	D			
DIRECT		04/05/88	P	
WELCH JOHN F JR	D			
DIRECT		04/11/88	H	
DIRECT		04/15/88	P	
INDIRECT		04/27/88		

SECURITY TRANSACTIONS AND HOLDINGS

| TRANSACTIONS | | | | Month end holdings of securities |
| Bought or otherwise acquired | | Sold or otherwise disposed of | | |
Amount	Price	Amount	Price	
		1,840	$54.25	
		30	$55.13	1,000
2,000	$52.38			4,000
2,587	$52.38			
		2,560	$54.00	33,583
		907	$54.38	32,676
5,000	$42.38			53,000
				1,223
100	$40.38			700
		880		
20,000	$39.63			107,266
				5,650

(table continues)

OFFICIAL SUMMARY OF

ISSUER SECURITY REPORTING PERSON NATURE OF OWNERSHIP	Relationship	Date of trans- action	Character	Late, amended or inconsistent
GENERAL HOST CORP				
COM				
HOORNSTRA EDWARD H	D			
DIRECT		04/07/88	S	
GENERAL INSTR CORP				
COM				
HOFFMAN RICHARD M	O			
DIRECT		04/08/88	S	
INDIRECT		04/08/88	U	
SHUH FREDERICK	C			
DIRECT		04/11/88	T	
DIRECT		04/11/88	X	
GENERAL MICROWAVE CORP				
COM				
GRAND BERNARD	O			
DIRECT		05/23/86	D	
DIRECT		10/30/87	P	L
DIRECT		11/02/87	P	L

SECURITY TRANSACTIONS AND HOLDINGS

Bought or otherwise acquired		Sold or otherwise disposed of		Month end holdings of securities
Amount	Price	Amount	Price	
		100,000	$10.00	220,721
		14,833	$35.63	18,000
		810		
19,200	$11.32			43,854
11,854	$21.40			
1,055				23,161
1,000	$6.25			24,161
1,000	$6.25			

Total amount of General Electric *sib* during period: $1,009,000.

successive "P" entries in Official Summary

Observe that the companies with *sib* stand out clearly to a scanner of *Official Summary*, as illustrated by the examples on the preceding pages 30–85. By simply going through *Official Summary* once a month with an eye for columns of associated successive "P" entries, one easily finds the *sib* stocks.

linkage between sib and subsequent upward price movement for certain NYSE issues

The fourteen examples shown on pp. 30–85 represent only a fraction of the stocks with *sib* in these issues of *Official Summary*. In fact, an additional screening filter has been applied to the *sib* stocks in selecting the latter fourteen examples— they are all listed and traded on the NYSE. The reason for restricting consideration to issues traded on the NYSE is empirical and practical: while there exists a salient statistical linkage between stock price movement and previously reported insider buying for a class of stocks listed and actively traded on the NYSE, no similar statistical linkage has been uncovered for any simply delineated class of stocks traded elsewhere.

Most NYSE stocks are indeed "a breed apart," as a brokerage firm might put it. Representing the upper tier of United States corporations in terms of products, financial strength, and quality of management, there are over 1500 common stocks on the NYSE with more than 50 billion shares traded annually. The market value of NYSE shares, currently about $2 trillion, is roughly half the GNP (the value of all goods and services produced annually in the United States). The regulations for maintenance of a NYSE listing require standard accounting practices according to Hoyle, with quarterly and annual reports that contain more detailed and comprehensive financial information for present and prospective shareholders. In addition, the greater visibility, liquidity, and following of most NYSE stocks, coupled with the high standards for proper auction trading by NYSE specialists (brokers who specialize in setting the bid-ask prices of stocks and actually executing buy and sell orders) work to promote more appropriate price movements. During and in the aftermath recovery period that followed the general stock market panic of October 1987, NYSE issues had price movements with much less evi-

*special features
of NYSE stocks*

dent pathology than stocks traded on the AMEX or stocks traded by NASDAQ.[10] Of considerable relevance to such price action is the fact that NYSE issues are the vehicles of choice for most institutional investors. Here *institutional* refers to banks, pension and mutual funds, college endowments, insurance companies, and the like — the big buyers and sellers who dominate the present stock markets. Since the buying and selling of stocks by institutional investors is the principal driving force for price change, it is not surprising that the class of equities preferred by institutions manifest a special relationship between legally reported insider buying and stock price movement.

institutions: banks, funds, and the like

institutional preference for NYSE issues

For the purpose of using *sib* as an aid in predicting stock price movement, one must restrict considerations to NYSE issues with at least *adequate visibility* and *satisfactory investment quality*.[11] Value Line Stock Reports, available as a useful reference in public and university libraries, cover most NYSE companies. If a NYSE company is one of the few not covered by Value Line (hence not appearing in the

need for adequate visibility and satisfactory investment quality

index list to the Reports), by definition the stock does not have adequate visibility and/or investment
quality.[12] Moreover, a NYSE issue
covered by Value Line but with a
low level of trading activity, say
typically less than 100,000 shares
(= 0.10 in our units of volume)
per week, does not have adequate
visibility. Since many security analysts and advisory services systematically review every NYSE issue on a
regular basis, low visibility is more
often a symptom of serious corporate
deficiencies than of Cinderella-type
neglect.

A NYSE stock will be dropped by
Value Line if its financial condition
deteriorates to the point where speculative uncertainties eclipse investment quality. Here balance sheet
and other venerable investment
quality criteria enter in a critical
manner.[13] If the company has publicly traded bonds, a recent Standard and Poor's Bond Guide enables
one to infer the financial strength
of the company through the rating
of its bonds. The rating of B is the
lowest that guarantees perpetuat-
ing visibility for the company, as it
is not unusual for Value Line and

*bond ratings: a
good indicator
of financial
strength*

other advisory services to drop or ignore companies with bonds that have slipped to a rating of CCC or worse.

Table 3 displayed below shows the relevant visibility and investment quality information for the NYSE *sib* companies excerpted from *Official Summary* on pp. 30–85. At the time that their *sib* occurred, twelve of the NYSE issues

Table 3. Visibility and Bond Ratings of Representative *sib* Companies

Company	Ticker Symbol	Value Line Coverage	Trading Activity >100,000 Sh/Wk	S & P Bond Ratings
Avon Products	AVC	Yes	Yes	BBB
BankAmerica	BAC	Yes	Yes	BBB
Bell Atlantic	BEL	Yes	Yes	AA
Kentucky Utilities	KU	Yes	Yes	AA
(Consolidated Stores	CNS	No	Yes	*)
GAF Corporation	GAF	Yes	Yes	B
CalMat	CZM	Yes	Yes	*
Lomas &Nettleton	LNF	Yes	Yes	BBB
(BRT Realty Trust	BRT	No	No	*)
Redman Industries	RE	Yes	Yes	*
Continental Illinois	CIL	Yes	Yes	BBB
Pier 1 Imports	PIR	Yes	Yes	B
Best Products	BES	Yes	Yes	B
General Electric	GE	Yes	Yes	AAA

* None traded publicly.

in the table satisfied the visibility and investment quality requirements prescribed above, but Consolidated Stores and BRT Realty Trust did not. It is noteworthy that just two monthly issues after *sib* appeared for Consolidated Stores (pp. 46-47), *Official Summary* showed heavy insider selling in this stock at prices below the *sib* level (pp. 92-95). Such a nullification of *sib* by insider selling just two or three months after the *sib* date is not uncommon for AMEX, NASDAQ or NYSE issues of lesser visibility and/or lower investment quality. The reason for this may be that smaller companies can suffer serious business reversals and disappointments in a short period of time. In any event, the misleading *sib* in *Official Summary* is well-correlated with stocks of lesser visibility and lower investment quality.

eliminating NYSE sib issues with inadequate visibility and/or lower investment quality

Henceforth, NYSE *sib* stocks with adequate visibility and satisfactory investment quality will be referred to as *sib+* stocks. Shown without parentheses in Table 3 on p. 90, the twelve *sib+* stocks are biased to have major upward price movements during the months and/or years that follow the significant insider buying

sib+ stocks

(From No. 9 of Vol. 53, received by subscribers on or about January 13, 1988)

OFFICIAL SUMMARY OF

ISSUER
  SECURITY
    REPORTING PERSON
      NATURE OF OWNERSHIP
	Relationship	Date of trans-action	Character	Late, amended or inconsistent

CONSOLIDATED RAIL ESOP	B			
DIRECT		10/31/87	U	
NEWMAN WILLIAM B JR	O			
DIRECT		10/01/87	B	
OWENS CLIFFORD W	O			
DIRECT		10/01/87	B	
SIMS MICHAEL D	O			
DIRECT		10/01/87	B	
WILLIAMS GERHARD M JR	O			
DIRECT		10/01/87	B	
CONSOLIDATED STORES CORP				
COM				
P				
SCHOTTENSTEIN CHAP TRUST #1	AF			
DIRECT		08/17/87	S	L
DIRECT		08/19/87	S	L
DIRECT		09/01/87	S	L
DIRECT		09/02/87	S	L
SCHOTTENSTEIN CHAP TRUST #2	AF			
DIRECT		08/17/87	S	L
DIRECT		08/19/87	S	L
DIRECT		09/01/87	S	L
DIRECT		09/02/87	S	L
SCHOTTENSTEIN CHAP TRUST #3	AF			
DIRECT		08/17/87	S	L
DIRECT		08/19/87	S	L
DIRECT		09/01/87	S	L
DIRECT		09/02/87	S	L
SCHOTTENSTEIN CHAP TRUST #4	AF			
DIRECT		08/17/87	S	L
DIRECT		08/19/87	S	L
DIRECT		09/01/87	S	L
DIRECT		09/02/87	S	L

SECURITY TRANSACTIONS AND HOLDINGS

TRANSACTIONS				Month end holdings of securities
Bought or otherwise acquired		Sold or otherwise disposed of		
Amount	Price	Amount	Price	
		10,304,617		40,153
277				277
301				301
306				306
276				276
		37,236	$7.13	
		2,283	$7.00	
		7,649	$7.38	
		61,173	$7.00	183,025
		19,173	$7.13	
		1,176	$7.00	
		3,940	$7.38	
		31,498	$7.00	94,242
		19,173	$7.13	
		1,176	$7.00	
		3,940	$7.38	
		31,498	$7.00	94,242
		19,173	$7.13	
		1,176	$7.00	
		3,940	$7.38	
		31,498	$7.00	94,242

(table continues)

OFFICIAL SUMMARY OF

ISSUER SECURITY REPORTING PERSON NATURE OF OWNERSHIP	Relationship	Date of trans-action	Character	Late, amended or inconsistent
SCHOTTENSTEIN DISC TRUST	AF			
DIRECT		08/17/87	S	L
DIRECT		08/19/87	S	L
DIRECT		09/01/87	S	L
DIRECT		09/02/87	S	L
SCHOTTENSTEIN JEROME M	AF			
DIRECT		08/11/87	S	L
DIRECT		08/17/87	S	L
DIRECT		08/17/87	S	L
DIRECT		08/17/87	S	L
DIRECT		08/18/87	S	L
DIRECT		08/19/87	S	L
DIRECT		09/01/87	S	L
DIRECT		09/01/87	S	L
DIRECT		09/02/87	S	L
DIRECT		09/02/87	S	L
DIRECT		09/02/87	S	L
INDIRECT		08/17/87	S	L
INDIRECT		08/17/87	S	L
INDIRECT		08/17/87	S	L
INDIRECT		08/19/87	S	L
INDIRECT		09/01/87	S	L
INDIRECT		09/01/87	S	L
INDIRECT		09/02/87	S	L
INDIRECT		09/02/87	S	L
INDIRECT		09/02/87	S	L
INDIRECT		09/02/87	S	L

SECURITY TRANSACTIONS AND HOLDINGS

TRANSACTIONS				Month end holdings of securities
Bought or otherwise acquired		Sold or otherwise disposed of		
Amount	Price	Amount	Price	
		21,460	$7.13	
		1,316	$7.00	
		4,407	$7.38	
		35,255	$7.00	105,480
		26,000	$8.63	
		54	$7.13	
		914	$7.38	
		44,656	$7.00	
		74,000	$7.00	
		2,797	$7.00	
		377	$7.38	
		8,996	$7.25	
		43	$7.25	
		959	$7.38	
		73,947	$7.00	
		7	$7.00	224,259
		233	$7.13	
		3,964	$7.38	
		193,584	$7.00	
		12,128	$7.00	
		1,634	$7.38	
		38,996	$7.25	
		188	$7.25	
		4,153	$7.38	
		320,554	$7.00	
		32	$7.00	972,152

Insider selling in Consolidated Stores.

Table 4. Pertinent Prices and Dates for Representative *sib+* Stocks

Ticker symbol	*Month/year and average price of sib*		*Approximate date Official Summary issue received by subscribers*
AVP	1/87	$26\frac{1}{2}$	5/21/87
BAC	3/87	$12\frac{1}{2}$	7/22/87
BEL	4/87	$64\frac{1}{2}$	8/12/87
KU	4/87	$18\frac{3}{4}$*	8/12/87
GAF	5/87	46	10/8/87
CZM	7/87	$29\frac{1}{4}$	10/29/87
LNF	9/87	$24\frac{7}{8}$	2/1/88
RE	11/87	$6\frac{1}{4}$	3/24/88
CIL	11/87	$2\frac{7}{8}$	3/24/88
PIR	1/88	6	4/15/88
BES	3/88	$11\frac{7}{8}$	8/5/88
GE	4/88	$40\frac{1}{4}$	8/5/88

*Adjusted for 2-for-1 split.

associated P-V graphics

reported in *Official Summary*. Such major upward price movements normally occur when the stock is bullish on a P-V graph, in the sense defined in Chapter III. A *sib+* stock is usually P-V bearish, for reasons discussed in Chapter IV, at the time the insiders do their buying, and the stock may or may not have turned P-V bullish by the time subscribers receive *Official Summary* and observe the *sib+* entry. In the

Table 4. (continued)

P-V condition of stock on latter date	Full price range following Official Summary reception date: Low-High to 10/21/88
↑	$19\frac{1}{4}$–$38\frac{5}{8}$
↓	$6\frac{5}{8}$–$17\frac{7}{8}$
↓	$60\frac{1}{2}$–$79\frac{3}{4}$
↓	15–$21\frac{1}{8}$
↓	$31\frac{3}{4}$–$65\frac{5}{8}$
↓	22–$46\frac{1}{8}$
↓	15–$22\frac{1}{4}$
↓	$6\frac{5}{8}$–$10\frac{1}{8}$
↓	$4\frac{1}{8}$–$5\frac{7}{8}$
↑	$8\frac{1}{2}$–$13\frac{3}{4}$
↑	$14\frac{1}{2}$–$26\frac{7}{8}$
↑	39–45

↑ means P-V bullish
↓ means P-V bearish

cases of the twelve *sib*+ stocks shown without parentheses in Table 3 on p. 90 and again in Table 4, four were P-V bullish and eight were P-V bearish on the dates that subscribers received the *Official Summary* issues with the respective *sib*+ entries.

If a *sib*+ stock is P-V bullish (↑) on the *Official Summary* reception date, the stock is strongly biased to continue its upward price

*price movement
of sib + stocks*

movement. For example, Avon Products (AVP) closed at $29\frac{3}{8}$ for the week ending 5/22/87, moved up strongly in the following weeks, and attained the 1987 high of $38\frac{5}{8}$ during the week ending 8/14/87 for a three-month price rise of 31.5%. On the other hand, if a *sib+* stock is P-V bearish on the *Official Summary* reception date, it may move lower and possibly afford an excellent buying opportunity below the *sib* price level, as evidenced by the price ranges shown in Table 4 on pp. 96-97 for the P-V bearish (↓) *sib+* examples. While additional insider buying in *sib+* stocks frequently appears in subsequent issues of *Official Summary*, about one out of ten *sib+* stocks shows subsequent selling in a dollar amount sufficient to nullify the previous statistical bias for upward price movement. Such a selling nullification occurred for only one of the twelve *sib+* examples in Table 4, namely GAF, as shown in the *Official Summary* excerpt on pp. 100-101. However, GAF had turned P-V bullish during the week ending 12/4/87, closing at 37. In the following weeks GAF moved up strongly to attain a post-Crash recovery high of $56\frac{3}{8}$ during the week

*insider selling
of sib + stocks*

ending 3/27/88 for a sixteen-week price rise of 52.4%. The climax of the latter price rise, during the week ending 3/27/88, coincided with the reception date for subscribers of the *Official Summary* issue which disclosed insider selling (pp. 100-101).

That the disclosure of insider transaction data in *Official Summary* can have an immediate impact on *sib+* stock price movement is also suggested by the price and volume figures for Pier 1 Imports (PIR) shown in Table 5 on p. 106. The pronounced jump in price and volume for PIR during the week ending 4/22/88 coincided with the reception of the *Official Summary* issue which disclosed the *sib* (pp. 74-77).

occasional price impact of sib+ on Official Summary reception date

The longer-term upward bias of a *sib+* stock is exemplified by Insilco (INR), an NYSE stock that had adequate visibility and satisfactory investment quality (bonds rated BBB by Standard & Poor's) when *sib* occurred in June 1985 at 19 (pp. 102-105). Three years later the insiders and other shareholders of INR received 31 in a cash buy out consummated in September 1988. Inclusive of

(From No. 1 of Vol. 54, received by subscribers on or about March 24, 1988)

ISSUER
  SECURITY
    REPORTING PERSON
      NATURE OF OWNERSHIP
	Relationship	Date of trans-action	Character	Late, amended or inconsistent

OFFICIAL SUMMARY OF				
GAF CORP				
COM				
BRENNAN JOHN A	O			
DIRECT		12/04/87	S	
HEYMAN SAMUEL J	D			
DIRECT		01/07/88		
INDIRECT		12/22/87	U	
INDIRECT		12/22/87	T	
GBI INTL INDS INC				
WT EXP				
MYERS SAM B JR	D			
INDIRECT		12/01/87	J	
GEICO CORP				
COM				
SISCO JOSEPH JOHN	D			
DIRECT		12/04/87	P	
GALAXY CARPET MLS INC				
COM				
FRENCH DURWOOD W	O			
DIRECT		12/29/87	T	
JACOBS DONALD P	D			
DIRECT		12/04/87	T	
INDIRECT		01/06/88		

SECURITY TRANSACTIONS AND HOLDINGS

| TRANSACTIONS | | | | Month end holdings of securities |
| Bought or otherwise acquired | | Sold or otherwise disposed of | | |
Amount	Price	Amount	Price	
		11,536	$36.50	1,250
				795,970
		274,600		
274,600				1,958,688
250,000				1
100	$94.50			1,500
500	$12.00			562
1,000	$10.25			3,156
				625

Insider selling and private disposition in GAF.

(From No. 7 of Vol. 51, received by subscribers on or about October 17, 1985)

OFFICIAL SUMMARY OF

ISSUER SECURITY REPORTING PERSON NATURE OF OWNERSHIP	Relationship	Date of trans-action	Character	Late, amended or inconsistent
HI CHICAGO TRUST	AF			
DIRECT		05/31/85	S	L
DIRECT		06/14/85	S	
KANTER BURTON W	D			
INDIRECT		05/03/85	3	L
THE HOLDING CO	AF			
DIRECT		05/31/85	S	L
INNOVEX INC				
COM				
TESSEM BERNT M	D			
DIRECT		06/03/85	K	
INDIRECT		06/03/85		
INSILCO CORP				
COM				
HARPER DONALD JACK	OD			
DIRECT		06/06/85	P	
INDIRECT		06/06/85		
MCLENDON JOHN A	OD			
DIRECT		06/06/85	P	
INDIRECT		06/06/85		
PETERSON GEORGE E	O			
DIRECT		06/06/85	P	
INDIRECT		06/06/85		
STILLMAN A EUGENE	O			
DIRECT		06/06/85	P	
DIRECT		06/06/85	P	

SECURITY TRANSACTIONS AND HOLDINGS

TRANSACTIONS				Month end holdings of securities
Bought or otherwise acquired		Sold or otherwise disposed of		
Amount	Price	Amount	Price	
		395	$12.25	8,895
		1,000	$12.25	7,895
				63,366
		825	$12.25	
		600	$13.00	
2,000	$19.00			17,259
				2,983
1,000	$19.00			4,295
				1,623
1,000	$19.00			11,080
				231
1,000				
1,000	$19.00			2,746

(table continues)

OFFICIAL SUMMARY OF

ISSUER
  SECURITY
    REPORTING PERSON
      NATURE OF OWNERSHIP
	Relationship	Date of trans-action	Character	Late, amended or inconsistent

WEBER JOHN J	O			
DIRECT		06/06/85	P	
INDIRECT		06/06/85		
WT EXP				
HARPER DONALD JACK	OD			
DIRECT		06/06/85	P	
MCLENDON JOHN A	OD			
DIRECT		06/06/85	P	
PETERSON GEORGE E	O			
DIRECT		06/06/85	P	
WEBER JOHN J	O			
DIRECT		06/06/85	P	
INSITUFORM EAST INC				
COM				
LANG ARTHUR G III	OD			
DIRECT		06/03/85	S	
DIRECT		06/07/85	S	
DIRECT		06/10/85	S	
DIRECT		06/11/85	S	
DIRECT		06/12/85	S	
DIRECT		06/13/85	S	
DIRECT		06/17/85	S	
DIRECT		06/21/85	S	
DIRECT		06/26/85	S	
DIRECT		06/28/85	S	

SECURITY TRANSACTIONS AND HOLDINGS

TRANSACTIONS				Month end holdings of securities
Bought or otherwise acquired		Sold or otherwise disposed of		
Amount	Price	Amount	Price	
100	$19.00			322
				132
2,000	$2.75			2,000
1,000	$2.75			1,000
1,000	$2.75			1,000
100	$2.75			100
		22,500	$8.07	
		2,500	$7.88	
		5,000	$8.00	
		2,700	$8.13	
		2,300	$8.50	
		1,000	$7.75	
		5,000	$9.63	
		10,000	$9.75	
		5,000	$9.13	
		12,000	$9.75	310,466

Total amount of Insilco *sib* during period: $116,000.

Table 5. Prices and Volume for PIR from 2/29/88 to 7/15/88

Week ending	Sales 100's	High	Low	Close	Change
3/4	1211	$8\frac{1}{4}$	$7\frac{3}{8}$	8	$-\frac{1}{8}$
3/11	3060	$8\frac{1}{8}$	7	$7\frac{3}{8}$	$-\frac{5}{8}$
3/18	2013	$7\frac{3}{4}$	$7\frac{1}{4}$	$7\frac{1}{2}$	$+\frac{1}{8}$
3/25	2740	$8\frac{1}{8}$	$7\frac{1}{2}$	$7\frac{3}{4}$	$+\frac{1}{4}$
4/1	3073	$8\frac{1}{2}$	$7\frac{5}{8}$	$8\frac{1}{2}$	$+\frac{3}{4}$
4/8	5270	$8\frac{7}{8}$	$8\frac{1}{8}$	$8\frac{7}{8}$	$+\frac{3}{8}$
4/15	5826	$9\frac{1}{8}$	$8\frac{1}{4}$	$8\frac{5}{8}$	$-\frac{1}{4}$
4/22	21,965	$11\frac{1}{4}$	$8\frac{1}{2}$	$10\frac{3}{4}$	$+2\frac{1}{8}$
4/29	16,686	$12\frac{1}{4}$	$10\frac{1}{2}$	12	$+1\frac{1}{4}$
5/6	10,033	$12\frac{1}{2}$	11	$12\frac{1}{8}$	$+\frac{1}{4}$
5/13	9271	$12\frac{5}{8}$	$11\frac{3}{8}$	$11\frac{3}{4}$	$-\frac{3}{8}$
5/20	3793	$11\frac{3}{8}$	$10\frac{7}{8}$	$11\frac{3}{8}$	$-\frac{3}{8}$
5/27	3606	$12\frac{1}{8}$	11	$12\frac{1}{8}$	$+\frac{3}{4}$
6/5	5139	$12\frac{3}{8}$	$11\frac{1}{2}$	12	$-\frac{1}{8}$
6/12	4002	12	$11\frac{3}{8}$	$11\frac{5}{8}$	$-\frac{3}{8}$
6/19	6335	$12\frac{1}{8}$	$11\frac{1}{4}$	12	$+\frac{3}{8}$
6/26	6189	$11\frac{7}{8}$	$11\frac{1}{2}$	$11\frac{3}{4}$	$-\frac{1}{4}$
7/1	5272	$12\frac{1}{8}$	$11\frac{1}{2}$	12	$+\frac{1}{4}$
7/8	14,508	13	12	13	$+1$
7/15	32,603	$13\frac{3}{4}$	$9\frac{3}{4}$	$10\frac{1}{8}$	$-2\frac{7}{8}$

typical multi-year performance of a sib+ stock

regular cash and stock dividends, the total return for the INR insiders was approximately 28% per annum from June 1985 to September 1988. In October 1985 and during other P-V bearish interludes in 1986, 1987, and early 1988, INR had downward movements that carried the price below 19 (falling to 14 in October 1987). Thus, investors

were afforded excellent opportuni-
ties for a substantially higher total
return by purchasing the stock below
the *sib* price.

NOTES

1. Welling, Kathryn M., "The Smart Money," *Barron's Busi-
   ness and Financial Weekly* , Sept. 12, 1988, pp. 11–36.
2. Kent, William A., *The Smart Money* . New York: Double-
   day, 1972, especially pp. 3–11.
3. Pratt, Shannon P. and Charles W. DeVere, *Insider
   Trading and Market Returns*, Portland State University,
   Sept. 1968, unpublished but reviewed by: Fosback, N. G. ,
   Stock Market Logic, Ft. Lauderdale, Florida: Institute for
   Econometric Research, 1985, pp.236–239; Moran, Mark
   J., *Insider Trading in the Stock Market*, St. Louis, MO:
   Center for the Study of American Business, Washington
   University, 1984. The latter work contains an interesting
   discussion on the informational advantages enjoyed by
   insiders on pp. 5–10.
4. Romeo, Peter J. and Michael D. Lefever, *Section 16 of
   the Securities Exchange Act of 1934, Securities Transactions by Statutory Insiders*, San Francisco: Corporate Counsel, 1986; Schrapp, James H., *Liability for
   Insider Trading under the Federal Securities Laws, New
   York: Practising Law Institute, 1978. That "informed"*
   insiders are usually free to trade their company's stock
   without violating the public disclosure of information
   provision in the Act of 1934 has been emphasized by
   Frome, R. L. and V. M. Rosenzweig, *Sales of Securities by Corporate Insiders*, New York: Practising
   Law Institute, 1975, pp. 159–161: "The distinction
   between fact and opinion for purposes of determining
   what information must be disclosed under Rule 10b-
   5 is often a difficult one to make. 'Educated guess-
   es', 'informed opinions' and 'reliable predictions' cannot

strictly be classified as hard facts ... Generally, it is difficult to determine whether a given piece of information is material without examining additional facts and circumstances surrounding the transaction."

5. Manne, Henry G., *Insider Trading and the Stock Market*, New York: Free Press, 1966, pp. 67–75. Writing with prophetic insight in the mid-'Sixties, this author intimated that the illegal use of insider information by affiliated persons involved a number of standard mechanisms, for example: "The special relationship of investment bankers, underwriters, and large brokerage houses to the American corporation has long been a subject of controversy, analysis, and even litigation. These multifaceted organizations ... are financial advisers, management counselors, ... merger arrangers, underwriters, and many other things. They may be, in addition, the clearinghouses par excellence for valuable [insider] information."

6. Gottschalk, Earl C., "Insider Stock Transactions are Challenged as a Market Indicator by New Research," *The Wall Street Journal* , Jan. 19, 1988, p. 31.

7. It is, of course, conceivable that several officers and/or directors might make and report large-size purchases of their stock merely because they expect investors who follow insider trading to buy later at higher prices. Such unscrupulous collusion by insiders is unlikely to occur in the formally structured ranks of the more visible, investment-grade NYSE companies.

8. *Official Summary* is available in university and some public libraries. One can subscribe to this periodical by telephoning (202) 275–3054 or writing to the Superintendent of Documents, U. S. Government Printing Office, Washington, D. C. 20402.

9. See references listed in Note 3.

10. In the wake of the Crash of October 1987 two specialists, one at the NYSE and the other at the AMEX, had fatal heart attacks and arrived almost simultaneously at the gate to Hell. Attached to the gate there was a telephone

and a sign stating, "You are Allowed One Telephone Call." They decided that in view of the crisis it would be best to telephone their respective exchanges and have their trading responsibilities covered. The AMEX specialist put his quarter in the slot, reached the AMEX and relayed the sad news. The NYSE specialist put his quarter in the slot, dialed the NYSE number, but instead reached an AT&T operator who requested $23.75 for the phone call. "But my AMEX colleague just made his phone call to Wall Street for only 25¢," stammered the NYSE specialist. "Yes," replied the operator, "the AMEX is currently a local number."

11. The "quality of insiders," a more subjective and problematic screening filter proposed recently by others (see note 1), may actually be correlated with adequate visibility and satisfactory investment quality for companies listed on the NYSE.

12. The reasons for Value Line excluding a NYSE company are usually very sound. In some cases such an exclusion may be due to financial weakness, while in other cases to the newness of the company's niche in its marketplace and the uncertain viability of its operations.

13. For example, see Clairmont, G. B. and K. Sokoloff, *Street Smart Investing*, New York: Random House, 1983.

3

P-V GRAPHS

Obviously stocks move up or down
because of aggressive buying or selling, in response or in anticipation of
good or bad news and good or bad
business conditions for the under-
lying companies. Owing to the lin-
gering influence of previous news
and the persistence of favorable
or unfavorable business conditions,
good or bad expectations are usually maintained on a time scale of
several months. When this happens,

price trends

individual stocks trend upward or downward for several (typically from three to nine) months[1] with relatively small intermediate reverse movements in price, corrections of less than 10% that interrupt the major movement. A stock is *bullish* if its price has held at or above the recent low and commenced or established an upward trend in which each successive intermediate decline holds at or above the previous intermediate low. A stock is *bearish* if its price has remained below the recent high and commenced or established a downward trend in which each successive intermediate advance falters at or below the previous intermediate high.

bullish

bearish

Quite clearly, the latter qualitative and more or less conventional definitions[2] of *bullish* and *bearish* become ambiguous at market tops and bottoms, when a stock goes from bullish to bearish or vice versa. To arrive at definitions that are more precise and thus useful in situations of trend reversal, one must consider a stock's transaction volume in addition to its price. The relationship between changes in price and changes in volume has been

price-volume relationship

understood in a rough intuitive fashion for many decades,[3] but only recently has the price-volume relationship been elucidated in a more precise manner with detailed mathematical studies.[4-8] By distilling the useful essence from the latter investigations, one is led to consider price-volume or *P-V graphs*, the most practical tool for assaying whether a stock is bullish or bearish at any time of interest. In particular, P-V graphs engender quantitative definitions of *bullish* and *bearish* that apply without ambiguity at market tops and bottoms, and thereby reveal changes in the condition of a stock at critical junctures.

at tops and bottoms

Figure 1 on p. 12 displays an elementary short-term P-V graph, showing AT&T common for the first three weeks of 1988. The price P is along the vertical axis (in dollars per share) and the cumulative volume V, the total number of shares traded up to the time of interest, appears along the horizontal axis (in millions of shares). Weekly volume and price data given above the figure are plotted by invoking a continuous, piecewise-constant slope approximation for P

elementary short-term P-V graph example

versus V. Notice that the continuous line with straight segments runs from the 1987 close of 27, to the first week's high of $29\frac{3}{8}$, to the first week's close of $27\frac{3}{4}$, to the second week's low of $26\frac{3}{4}$, etc., in a manner that minimizes the number of kinks (i.e., points at which the slope changes) in the P versus V approximation.

long-term graph example for sib+ stock

A much longer-term P-V graph is displayed in Figure 6 on p. 120, showing P versus V for the *sib+* stock CalMat (CZM) from 10/12/87 to 6/3/88. With the *Official Summary* reception date for the issue that showed the *sib* (about 10/29/87, see Table 4 on p. 96) corresponding to the $V = 1.2$ on the cumulative volume axis, this eight-month P-V graph presents somewhat more than a full bear-bull cycle for CZM. Observe that the volume of shares traded from the market peak at $P = 37\frac{1}{2}$ and $V = .20$ to the market nadir at $P = 22$ and $V = 1.92$ is labeled ΔV (pronounced "delta vee") and shown in the lower left corner of the graph. Like the distance legend on a map, ΔV is the key scale gauge employed in the interpretation of P-V graphs, and hence the value for

definition of ΔV

ΔV, the "selloff" volume in millions of shares traded in the most recent major decline of the stock, should always appear in the figure caption of a P-V graph. In the case of CZM for the time frame shown in Figure 6, the value $\Delta V = 1.72$ ($= 1.92 - .20$) is noted in the caption. Also observe that in the major decline from the $P = 37\frac{1}{2}$ peak to the $P = 22$ nadir, new intermediate lows were attained successively with the incremental change in V from new low to new low always less than the incremental change in V from the peak to the first low in the pair considered. In defining a new low (or new high), a slight penetration of a previous low (or high) by a fraction of a point is viewed as a successful test of the low (or high) and thus not counted as *new*. For example, in the case of the successive intermediate lows at $V = 1.18$ (with $P = 26$) and $V = 1.92$ (with $P = 22$), the incremental change in V amounted to .74, while the incremental change in V from the peak to the first low was .98. This exemplifies a general empirical feature of major declines for *sib+* stocks on P-V graphs: the incremental change in V from a low to a successive low is generally less

significance of ΔV in a major decline of a sib+ stock than the incremental change in V from the peak to the first low in the pair considered.

The definitions of *bullish* and *bearish* can now be sharpened in a quantitative fashion. A stock is *P-V bullish* if its price has held at or above the recent low for a volume greater than ΔV and commenced or established an upward trend in which each successive intermediate decline holds at or above the previous intermediate low. A stock is *P-V bearish* if its price has remained below the recent high for a volume ΔV and commenced or established a downward trend in which each successive intermediate advance falters at or below the previous intermediate high. According to these quantitative definitions, CZM turned P-V bullish at $P=30$ and $V=3.64$ (because $1.92 + \Delta V = 3.64$), remained P-V bullish as the price advanced to 46 at $V=5.11$, and then turned P-V bearish at $V=6.83$ (by virtue of $5.11 + \Delta V = 6.83$) with $P=41$. At every point in this bear-bull cycle for CZM, the P-V bullish and bearish definitions provided accurate predictors for the subsequent stock movement (in view of

definition of P-V bullish

definition of P-V bearish

pertinency of definitions over a full cycle

the additional fact that the price declined to below 30 in the months that followed the period on the P-V graph).

Figure 4 on p. 16 displays the P-V graph for the *sib+* stock Lomas and Nettleton Financial (LNF) from 2/1/88 to 7/8/88, the twenty-three week period following reception of the *Official Summary* issue that showed the *sib* (see p. 96). On volume $\Delta V = 42.8$, LNF declined in a persistent fashion from $39\frac{1}{4}$ in March 1987 to 15 in February 1988, with the latter nadir appearing at $V = 2.8$ in Figure 4. Hence, although LNF held above 15 during the period shown, the stock still remained P-V bearish because the volume after $V = 2.8$ had not yet exceeded $\Delta V = 42.8$; if the stock continued to hold above 15 through $V = 45.6$ ($= 2.8 + \Delta V$) and commenced or established an uptrend, it would then be classified as P-V bullish. As is typical for a stock in a P-V bearish condition, the pseudobullish rally from $V = 5.1$ to $V = 10.35$ featured intermediate movements of increasing slope up to the abortive peak at $22\frac{1}{4}$, before a swift and virtually complete retrenchment occurred.

P-V bearish sib+ example

In connection with the price-volume history of LNF shown in Figure 4, it is interesting to note that one can construct a *Rosetta stone* for interpreting the sequences of sloped line segments that constitute the intermediate price movements on a P-V graph. The most elementary Rosetta stone might be as pictured on p. 119 in Figure 5, with appropriate labels affixed. These interpretations of the sequences of sloped line segments on a P-V graph simply derive from the empirical fact that steady or expanding volume is necessary to sustain an up or down price movement, while contracting volume countervails an up or down price movement. A more elaborate Rosetta stone (useful for short-term trading purposes) can be fashioned by the reader after studying examples of P-V graphs.

Figure 7 on p. 121 displays the P-V graph for the *sib+* stock Pier 1 Imports (PIR) from 2/29/88 to 7/15/88, a period corresponding to the price-volume data on p. 106. After declining from $14\frac{5}{8}$ in July to $4\frac{3}{4}$ in October on volume $\Delta V = 4.9$, PIR turned P-V bullish in December 1987. On the reception date 4/15/88 for the *Official Summary*

Figure 5.   Basic Rosetta Stone for P-V Graphs

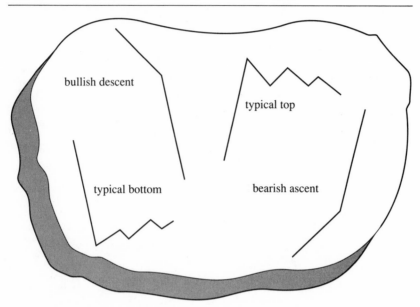

bullish descent

typical top

typical bottom

bearish ascent

issue that showed the *sib* (see p. 96), PIR closed at $8\frac{5}{8}$ with $V = 1.5$ in Figure 7. This stock advanced strongly in the following weeks, in a typical *sib*+ P-V bullish fashion, attained the high of $12\frac{1}{4}$ at $V = 6.0$ and then engaged in a side-wise price movement. Since the price remained below 12 and a fraction for a subsequent volume $\Delta V = 4.9$, PIR turned P-V bearish at $V = 10.9$. A final surge of speculative buying carried the price to a new high.

example of a P-V bullish to bearish transition

In contrast to the former examples, the P-V graph for Best Products

Figure 6.   CZM from 10/12/87 to 6/3/88 ($\Delta V = 1.72$ from $37\frac{1}{2}$ to 22)

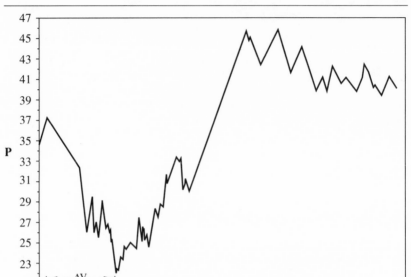

---

example of a
uniformly P-V
bullish graph
for a sib+ stock

(BES) from 4/25/88 to 9/30/88 displayed as Figure 8 on p. 123 is uniformly bullish. After declining from 13 in August to 6 in October on volume $\Delta V = 7.4$, BES turned P-V bullish in January 1987 and remained such prior to and through the period shown in the P-V graph. On the reception date 8/5/88 for the *Official Summary* issue that showed the *sib* (see p. 96), BES had already moved up substantially to close at $14\frac{1}{2}$ and $V = 10.6$ in Figure 8. This stock continued to maintain a P-V bullish condition even after attain-

Figure 7.   PIR from 2/29/88 to 7/15/88 ($\Delta V = 4.9$ from $14\frac{5}{8}$ to $4\frac{3}{4}$)

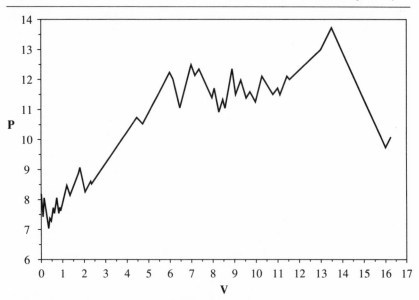

ing the intermediate high of $16\frac{5}{8}$ at $V = 17.0$, for the latter high was surpassed at $V = 23.6$ (less than 17.0 + $\Delta V = 24.4$).

Figure 9 on p. 124 displays the P-V graph for the *sib+* stock General Electric (GE) from 4/25/88 to 9/23/88. GE had declined from $66\frac{3}{8}$ in August 1987 to 39 in the week ending 12/4/87 on volume $\Delta V = 186$. During the interim between the week ending 12/4/87 and the 4/25/88 starting date for Figure 9, the stock held above 39 and transacted a cumulative

another example of P-V bearish to bullish transition for a sib+ stock

volume of 161. Hence, GE was potentially P-V bullish at $V = 25$ ($= \Delta V - 161$) and $P = 40\frac{1}{2}$ in Figure 9, with the brief fractional-point penetration of 39 at $V = 17$ viewed as a successful test of the old low at 39 and not as a new low. In view of the rally and new intermediate high of $44\frac{3}{4}$ attained at $V = 68$, GE was P-V bullish when it closed at $41\frac{3}{4}$ on 8/5/88, corresponding to $V = 93$ in Figure 9, the reception date for the *Official Summary* issue that showed the *sib* (see p. 96).

examples of P-V graphs for lower priced sib+ stocks

As examples of P-V graphs for lower-priced *sib*+ stocks, Figures 10 and 11 on pp. 126 and 129 show Redman Industries (RE) and Continental Illinois (CIL) from 2/29/88 to 9/2/88. RE had declined on volume $\Delta V = 3.39$ from 12 in August 1987 to $5\frac{1}{4}$ in the week ending 12/13/87, while CIL had declined on volume $\Delta V = 26.1$ from $5\frac{7}{8}$ in July 1987 to $2\frac{1}{4}$ also in the week ending 12/13/87. Both stocks subsequently held above their nadirs of $5\frac{1}{4}$ and $2\frac{1}{4}$ prior to the starting date 2/29/88 for the P-V graphs, transacting volumes of 1.54 and 14.0 respectively during this interim period. For the week ending 3/25/88 when the *Official Summary* issue that showed the *sib* was

Figure 8.   BES from 4/25/88 to 9/30/88 ($\Delta V = 7.4$ from 13 to 6)

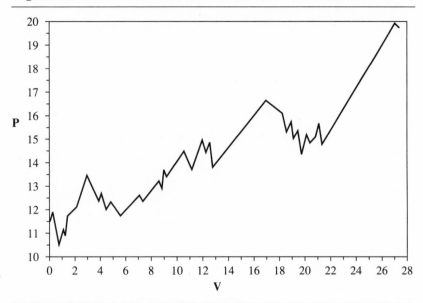

received by subscribers (see Table 4 on p. 96), RE closed at $7\frac{1}{4}$ and $V = .84$ in Figure 10, while CIL closed at $3\frac{3}{4}$ and $V = 2.4$ in Figure 11. These stocks turned P-V bullish at $V = 1.85$ ($= \Delta V - 1.54$) with $P = 7\frac{1}{8}$ and $V = 12.1$ ($= \Delta V - 14.0$) with $P = 5$, respectively. A continuation of RE's P-V bullish condition was indicated by the new intermediate high at $V = 4.53$ (less than $1.85 + \Delta V = 5.24$) and $P = 10\frac{1}{8}$, while CIL was already well entrenched in an upward movement through the latter part of the period covered by Figure 11.

Figure 9.   GE from 4/25/88 to 9/23/88 ($\Delta V = 186$ from $66\frac{3}{8}$ to 39)

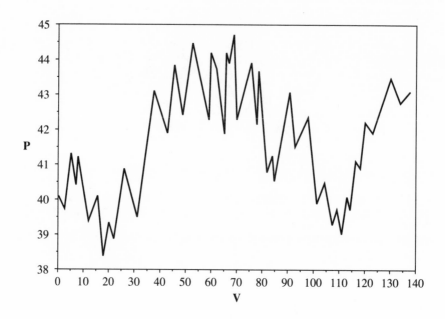

---

*manifestations
of informational
asymmetry in
P-V graphs*

To understand why P-V graphs work as generally reliable predictors for future stock price movement, one must consider the informational asymmetry that prevails in stock markets, a subject discussed further in Chapter IV. The basic aspect of informational asymmetry that enters into P-V graphs is believed to be the following. Because of what they know, better-informed market participants are inclined to buck the trend in making their buy and sell transactions[9], while lesser-informed market participants are nclined to buy and sell with the trend, being influenced and reassured by the collective movement. Thus when a stock turns P-V bullish or bearish, it means that better-informed market participants have produced a trend reversal with concerted buying or selling. This concerted buying or selling shows up in a P-V graph by a transaction volume that exceeds the "selloff" volume ΔV for the stock of interest while the price initiates the first phase of the new trend.

informational asymmetry and trend reversal

On a scale of order ΔV, several successive intermediate up or down price movements on a P-V graph will display a structure that can be identified and classified into one of several dynamical regimes. These regimes are analogous to the qualitatively distinct types of motion of a typical confined fluid, as shown in Figure 2 on p. 14, and the regimes for stock price movement can be given the same names as those for fluid motion. In fact, the analogy for stock

regimes of motion on a P-V graph

Figure 10.   RE from 2/29/88 to 9/2/88 ($\Delta V = 3.39$ from 12 to $5\frac{1}{4}$)

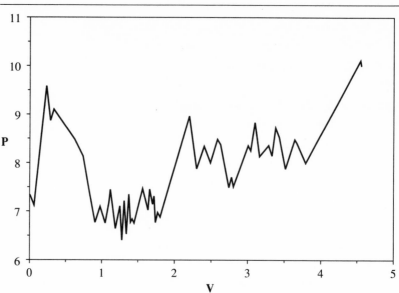

Rayleigh and Nusselt numbers as quantitative measures of risk in the fundamental and technical outlooks

---

price movement becomes customized and more intuitive if one views the Rayleigh and Nusselt numbers appearing as the physical parameters for the regimes of fluid motion in Figure 2 as mathematical quantities which capture and express the uncertainty or risk in both the fundamental and technical outlooks for a particular stock. By definition in this analogy, the *Rayleigh number* is a quantitative measure of the risk in the fundamental outlook and the *Nusselt number* is a quantitative measure of the risk in the technical outlook. Very thorough first-rate fundamental and technical analyses are supposed to go into determining the Rayleigh and Nusselt numbers respectively; while both quantities increase in magnitude with increasing risk, the Rayleigh and Nusselt numbers are given by separate and distinct (fundamental and technical) risk determinations for any particular stock.[10] However, because very thorough fundamental and technical analyses generally lead to valid assessments, the Rayleigh and Nusselt numbers are well correlated. That is, if each stock is plotted as a point on a Rayleigh versus Nusselt number *risk graph*, the points lie along a (somewhat curved) line, as shown in Figure 2. In the regimes of relatively small Rayleigh numbers, i.e., small risk in the fundamental and/or technical outlook, a stock's P-V graph has a more regular, periodic, and seemingly controlled character, like the *oscillation* shown for AT&T in Figure 1 on p. 12 and for GE in Figure 9 on p. 124—P-V graphics to be desired by risk averse investors. On the other hand, for moderate and relatively large Rayleigh numbers, corresponding to larger risk in the fundamental and/or technical outlook, a stock's P-V graph has an erratic, aperiodic

correlation between the quantitative measures of risk in the fundamental and technical outlooks

relation between risk and structure on a P-V graph

and stochastic (meaning randomlike) character, like the *chaos* shown for LNF in Figure 4 on p. 16. Table 6 displayed on p. 129 summarizes this relationship between the risk in the company's prospects and the structure on a P-V graph.[11]

It should be noted that longer-term P-V graphs usually show several contiguous regimes of motion, as the stock moves along the Rayleigh-Nusselt correlation line in Figure 2 with the passage of time and increasing or decreasing uncertainty in the company's prospects. Thus, for example, the P-V graph for CZM in Figure 6 on p. 120 shows *chaos* from about $V = 1.2$ to $V = 3.5$ (while the stock was P-V bearish) followed by *convection-oscillation* (while the stock was P-V bullish). The P-V graph for PIR in Figure 7 on p. 121 shows dominant *convection* up to about $V = 5.5$ followed by *oscillation* to about $V = 11$ and then *chaos*, successive regimes associated with increasing risk. The reverse sequence of *chaos* to *oscillation* to *convection* is shown in Figure 10 on p. 126 for RE as this stock turned from P-V bearish to P-V bullish. An alternation between *convection* and *oscillation* is evi-

changes in the regime of motion

convection, oscillation, and chaos

Table 6. Risk and Structure on a P-V Graph

	Rayleigh Number Regime	*Structure on a P-V Graph*
direction	*Convection*	more regular, periodic, and seemingly
of increasing risk	*Oscillation*	controlled intermediate movements
or uncertainty in	*Chaos*	erratic, aperiodic, and stochastic
the company's	*Transition*	intermediate movements, with the degree
prospects	*Soft Turbulence*	of incoherency increasing from *chaos* to
	Hard Turbulence	*hard turbulence*

Figure 11. CIL from 2/29/88 to 9/2/88 ($\Delta V = 26.1$ from $5\frac{7}{8}$ to $2\frac{1}{4}$)

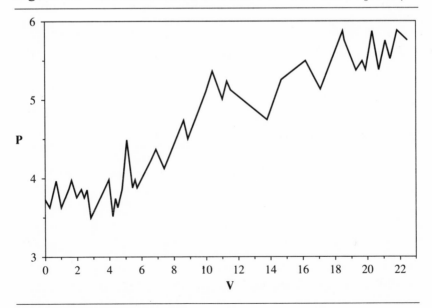

dent in the uniformly bullish P-V graph for BES shown as Figure 8 on p. 123. Finally, the P-V graph for CIL in Figure 11 on p. 129 shows a dominant *oscillation-convection* with a brief relapse to *chaos* in the vicinity of $V = 5$.

NOTES

1. Although it is unusual for a stock to maintain either a bullish or bearish condition for more than several months, the extraordinary general bull market of 1982–1987 and the Crash of 1987 have produced recent examples of longer-term bullish or bearish conditions. However, it should be noted that many well-known NYSE issues were bearish at different times during the 1980–1986 period and made their lows in years other than in 1982, as shown by the examples in the table below.

Name of Company	Ticker Symbol	Year of 1980–1986 Low	Price at 1980–1986 Low
Sears Roebuck	S	1980	$14\frac{3}{8}$
Chrysler	C	1981	$1\frac{3}{8}$[a]
Trans World Airlines	TWA	1983	$7\frac{1}{8}$
Amer. Tel. & Tel.	T	1984	$14\frac{7}{8}$
Eastman Kodak	EK	1985	41
USX	X	1986	$14\frac{1}{2}$

[a]Adjusted for subsequent stock split.

2. For example, Finley, Harold M., *Everybody's Guide to the Stock Market*, Chicago: H. Regnery, 1959.

3. See, for example, reference in note 2.

4. Epps, T. and M. L. Epps, "The Stochastic Dependence of Security Price Changes and Transaction Volumes," *Econometrica,* Vol. 44, March 1976, pp. 305–321.

5. Rogalski, R., "The Dependence of Price and Volume" *Review of Economics and Statistics,* May 1978, pp. 268–274.

6. Tauchen, G. and M. Pitts, "The Price Variability-Volume Relationship on Speculative Models," *Econometrica,* Vol. 51, March 1983, pp. 485–505.

7. Smirlock, M., and L. Starks, "A Further Examination of Stock Price Changes and Transaction Volume." *Journal of Financial Research,* Fall 1985, pp. 217–226.

8. Karpoff, J. M., "The Relation between Price Changes and Trading Volume," *Journal of Financial and Quantitative Analysis,* Vol. 22, March 1987, pp. 109–126.

9. Prominently successful and consistently better informed fund managers usually refer to themselves as *contrarians,* because they make bucking the trend a standard tactic in purchasing carefully selected stocks or in selling those that are overvalued. Members of this elite group of fund managers include Dean LeBaron (discussed in a feature article in the *Wall Street Journal* 12/8/84) and John Neff (discussed in a feature article in the *Philadelphia Inquirer* 10/2/88). While the term *contrarian* has a tactical basis in trend bucking, one must be better informed in order to be contrary and successful.

10. As peerless security analysts, the fundamentalist "Rayleigh" and the technician "Nusselt" made it their practice to present a quantitative assessment of the risk outlook in their stock reports.

11. The large Rayleigh number (high-risk) regimes of *transition, soft turbulence* and *hard turbulence* appear on P-V graphs for *sib*+ stocks only in rare instances (such as in October 1987) when general market conditions foster extremely erratic price movements. These regimes are basically intensifications of *chaos,* with the degree of incoherency increasing from *chaos* to *hard turbulence.*

4

ADDITIONAL PRACTICAL TENETS

My earliest memorable experience with corporate *imagery* took place when I was eight years old. On Monday, December 8, 1941, the day after the attack on Pearl Harbor, we heard that Japanese-Americans were being rounded up as suspected foreign agents. There were no Japanese-Americans in our neighborhood, but my friends and I were fond of Kato, who was the Green Hornet's resourceful compan-

corporate imagery in 1941

ion on the radio Tuesday and Thursday evenings. On Tuesday evening December 9, we all sat glued to the radio to see what would happen to Kato.

The program announcer had in the past always said, "And now the Green Hornet and his faithful Japanese valet Kato," but this night he said, "And now the Green Hornet and his faithful *Filipino* valet Kato." We looked at one another in relief —Kato's image had been quickly restored by *acquisition*. He was now a citizen of the friendly Philippines!

Did General MacArthur cut the red tape?

The rapid change of a corporate image by acquisition or otherwise has become commonplace, and one should never hesitate to buy an unpopular stock with a clouded image if it is *sib+* and P-V bullish. In fact, *sib* itself normally takes place in a fairly narrow price range, close to the stock's 12-month low and at a time when the company's public and Wall Street image is clouded by overtly negative factors. During the period of significant insider buying, it is not unusual for full-service brokerage firms and investment advi-

"Investors should look elsewhere for purchases."

sory services to ignore or classify the stock as "untimely for purchase," because there is no apparent reason which might provide logical justification for a general buy (or in some cases even a hold) recommendation. Often six months or more elapse from the time of *sib* to the time when favorable news is released or new and unexpected positive developments brighten the prospects for the company. As mentioned before, *sib* must occur well in advance of favorable news or positive corporate developments in order to be perfectly legal and proper according to federal law. It is this multi-month interval of time, after *sib* takes place and before favorable news or positive developments impact the stock price, that permits the *Official Summary* to play a timely and central role in the prediction of future price movements.

the necessary multi-month delay

Just as negative imagery must be taken lightly, positive imagery must be viewed with equivalent skepticism. Straining out valid and useful informational substance from imagery is extremely difficult, and in many cases impossible to do with any degree of confidence by an independent private investor. One must

"If it is not true, it is very well invented."
—Bruno

*"The market is
a place set apart
where people
may deceive
each other."
—Anacharsis*

*for our
shareholders*

therefore be wary of prognostications regarding a company's future performance, as provided by security analysts, brokerage firms, advisory services, and the corporation itself. In particular, one should distrust a glowing (tranquilizing) quarterly or annual report from a company after the stock has had a major advance in price. It would be easy to compile a large collection of rosy corporate forecasts which were released about the same time that the officers and directors sold large amounts of their company's stock, according to the *Official Summary*. For example, in a 1986 annual report that I received in March 1987, the CEO predicted a "sensational 1987" and concluded with the reassuring statement: "I believe that we have put in place the managerial, financial, and technical resources to meet [our] most fundamental goal—to create the maximum long-term value for our shareholders." But after receiving No. 4, Vol. 53 of the *Official Summary* in July 1987, I learned that this fellow and three of his corporate cronies had sold over $1 million worth of stock at about the same time that other shareholders were receiving the radiant annual report and possibly adding to their holdings with new purchases! If you are not automatically inclined to be skeptical when reading brokerage firm, advisory service, and corporate prognostications and pronouncements, you should not invest in stocks! For if picking stocks is akin to forecasting the winners in a beauty contest, as Keynes suggested, it's a beauty contest in which the contestants are permitted to wear veils!

in addition to Victorian swimsuits, of course

Corporate imagery is sustained by *informational asymmetry*—that some investors and traders know much more about the facts and figures pertinent to a company's prospects than other market participants. Pervasive in all areas of social and intellectual activity,[1] informational asymmetry in securities markets has been the subject of several scholarly and noteworthy investigations.[2-6] Enscounced at the top of the information scale for market participants are the corporate insiders, defined according to the SEC on p. 22. While it is evident that the insiders of an investment quality NYSE company may not be aware of all factors that will effect the corporation's profitability or shareholder

"Benignant information is his hobby."
—A. Guiterman

value, they are nevertheless often privy to important information (see p. 23) that is either deemed to be proprietary or confidential for legalistic reasons. It has been commonly known for many years that officers and directors often have a secret and more accurate balance sheet which is markedly different from the balance sheet released to the financial media and to stockholders.[7] Such information remains in the exclusive province of the insiders and may motivate their buying and selling of the company's stock.

private balance sheets

Some distance down on the information scale are influential security analysts and associated institutional portfolio managers, the members of the *analyst-institution symbiosis* who direct the buying and selling of most of the 50 billion shares traded annually on the NYSE. The institutions pay the analysts' fees, and in return the analysts are obliged to seek prudent and optimally profitable channels for institutional investment, principally in large-capitalization equity and debt vehicles. The institutional need to take large positions in stocks causes the analysts to ignore com-

analyst-institution symbiosis

panies which have smaller market capitalizations.[8] Moreover, a lack of up-to-date positive information pertinent to a large-capitalization stock increases the perceived risk and thus dampens the analyst-institutional interest. In the cases of either small or large companies, the hallmark of analyst-institutional neglect is a relatively low P/E (price to earnings ratio). On the other hand, analyst interest and institutional holdings in certain stocks can tend to snowball with the release of positive information over a period of time, because there is a continual need for institutions to invest cash, and an analyst is most secure when he or she reiterates a buy or sell decision made previously by other analysts. Hence, the analyst-institution symbiosis causes certain stocks to be neglected (and depressed in price with a relatively low P/E) and other stocks to be limelighted (and elevated in price with a relatively high P/E) to an extent well in excess of informational evaluations.

low P/E: the hallmark of analyst-institutional neglect

The private investor can utilize the analyst-institution symbiosis, and the concomitant tendency for certain stocks to snowball in

S&P Stock Guide issue	Aug. '86	April '87	Feb. '88
No. Institutions holding CZM	51	69	79

Copyright© Standard & Poor's, 1986-1988.

detecting the trend in analyst-institution interest

popularity, by monitoring the number of institutions that hold a stock of interest on a month-to-month basis. For example, in the case of the *sib+* stock CalMat (CZM), the monthly issues of Standard and Poor's Stock Guide showed that the number of institutions holding CZM increased monotonically from mid-1986 through early 1988 (see table above). The likelihood of a major upward price movement in CZM after the stock turned P-V bullish in February 1988 (see discussion on pp. 114-116) was enhanced by this previous increase in the number of institutions with CZM in their portfolios.[9]

"The folly of one person is the fortune of another."
—Bacon

At the bottom of the information scale (see Figure 12 on p. 141) are rank speculators, a group of minor significance for investment quality NYSE issues. With regard to their positioning at the base of the information scale, it should be noted that some rank speculators do not even know the

Figure 12. Information Scale for Market Participants in an Investment Quality NYSE Issue

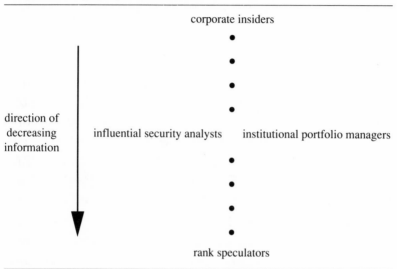

corporate insiders

direction of decreasing information

influential security analysts   institutional portfolio managers

rank speculators

line of business of the company when they elect to buy or sell the stock entirely on the basis of tape action. To these speculators, "information" is the name of the company that goes with the ticker symbol!

All other market participants, investors, traders, and speculators with access to various amounts and quality of information and hence with very different opinions or feelings regarding the future prospects of the company, are distributed from top to bottom over the information scale, shown in Figure 12 for

"As many opinions as men."
—Terence

an investment quality NYSE issue. Because of this broad-based informational asymmetry, there are potential buyers and potential sellers of a stock at virtually any price level.

in making a long story short

While it originates at the top with the insiders' need to be proprietary and legalistic, and is therefore basically intentional, informational asymmetry is exacerbated by the fact that corporate officers and directors must simplify and condense relevant facts and figures, with estimated probabilities of occurrence omitted, in describing their current and projected situations to security analysts.[10] Furthermore, an analyst's subjective evaluation of this incomplete information is conditioned in part by his or her past recommendations, the need to be consistent with such earlier evaluations, and the analyst-institution symbiosis. Thus, numerous extraneous factors enter before full-service brokerage firms and advisory services arrive at a buy, hold, or sell recommendation for a stock. The private investor should be aware of such informational obscurations in viewing a buy, hold, or sell recommendation by a security analyst,

the straight-jacket of past pronouncements

full-service brokerage firm, or advisory service.

Informational fallibilities are obviously inherent in the fundamental analysis performed by security analysts, but it would make no sense for a private investor to attempt his or her own fundamental analysis by studying a company's published reports, balance sheet financial data, and product line with the goal of forecasting earnings. The private investor should view fundamental analysis as something done by professionals (with varying accuracy) and already incorporated into the current stock price by the unrelenting pressures of institutional buying and selling. Included under the heading of fundamental analysis, and thus taken into account completely by the current stock price, are such venerable items as the earnings history and earnings forecasts for the company, the current dividend[11] yield, the debt-to-equity ratio,[12] the book value,[13] and even the CEO's taste (or lack of) in men's or women's fashions! In summary, the current price of an actively traded investment quality NYSE issue thoroughly discounts

fundamental analysis

stock pricing efficiency
—with regard to the past and the commonly expected future

*the impact
of the
unexpected*

and sums up in one figure the entire past history and expected outlook for the company as judged by astute Wall Street professionals. Only unexpected future developments and unanticipated news, perhaps related to currently concealed information, can impact the future stock price and drive it up or down in a significant manner.

Included in the category of unexpected future developments are changes in the general economic outlook and the broader stock market tonality, as reflected in the Dow-Jones Industrial Average (or "Dow" for short), the index that is fairly well coupled to the waxing and waning of anticipations for general business activity. Here Sharpe's relation (see p. 4)

$$\ln P = \alpha + \beta \ln P_M$$

*"Dowager"—one
who invests
simply on the
basis of
Sharpe's
equation*

may assume practical relevance, for the theoretical increase in α ("alpha") that a P-V bullish *sib+* stock would normally accrue (thus increasing its P) can be completely negated by a decrease in P_M, the "price of the market" represented by the Dow. It is customary in employing Sharpe's equation to make the mathematical definition that β ("beta," given in

S&P and Value Line stock reports) is a fixed constant for any stock, determined by its most recent 12-month price history. Therefore, if α doesn't increase fast enough, a stockholder is at the mercy of the Dow because of the $\beta \ln P_M$ term in Sharpe's equation.

Bull and bear markets for the Dow often run for many months or several years as prevalent optimism or pessimism about future business conditions holds sway. With pessimism widespread in August 1982, the Dow made a bear market nadir at 776 before initiating a remarkable five-year bull market.[14] Optimism regarding future business conditions and the future course of the general stock market was well entrenched in August 1987, when the Dow peaked at 2722 and advisory services such as Value Line continued to recommend fully invested positions and projected the Dow to surpass 3000 or 3200 by December 1987.

"From the sublime to the ridiculous is but a step."
—Napoleon

As is well known, the Federal Reserve has the power to alter the Dow trend by affecting changes in interest rates, because business expansion (or contraction) depends critically on the cost of bor-

influence of the Fed

rowed funds, and lending institutions respond quickly to cues
from the Federal Reserve. When
interest rates start to decline
after a sustained rise for several
years, or when the Federal Reserve
announces an unanticipated reduction in the discount rate (for funds
borrowed by member banks in the
Federal Reserve System), an upward
trend in the Dow usually develops
and persists as long as interest rates
continue to decline or remain steady.
When an interest-rate trend reversal and cyclical rise finally occurs,
a downward trend in the Dow usually follows within a period of several months.

interest rates:
1982–1987

The Dow upward trend that began
in August 1982 was initiated by
a sudden reduction in the discount
rate by the Federal Reserve, at a
time when interest rates were very
close to their all-time peaks, e.g., 30-
year Treasury bonds priced to yield
about 15%. Interest rates declined
during the bull market and reached
cyclical lows in the latter half of
1986, with 30-year Treasury bonds
priced to yield about $7\frac{1}{4}\%$. The cyclical rise in interest rates commenced
in February 1987 and accelerated

through the spring of 1987 (30-year Treasury bonds yielding about 9% in late May), and hence the imminence of a decline in the general market had been signaled three months before the Dow attained its historic high of 2722 in August 1987. The persistent rise in interest rates preconditioned the supersized panic selloff on October 19, which was throttled only when the Federal Reserve did a rapid about-face and moved to reduce interest rates on October 20. Clearly the perceived trend in interest rates, as orchestrated by the Federal Reserve, has a powerful effect on the trend of the Dow.

The dominant idea that guides Federal Reserve policy in regulating interest rates is the *avoidance of economic extremes* — maintenance of a mildly inflationary, and hence prospering, domestic economy with the dollar subject to appropriate, orderly revaluations against the currencies of our economic partners throughout the world. As long as it does not threaten to destabilize the dynamic equilibrium of the system (as it threatened in October 1987), the status of the stock market is ordi-

guiding philosophy of the Fed

narily given a low priority when the Federal Reserve considers revisions in interest rate policy. In acting to avoid economic extremes, the Federal Reserve will be inclined to lower interest rates when pessimism in business and financial circles becomes pronounced, and raise interest rates when optimism becomes excessive. Here *pessimism* and *optimism* are quantified by the key relevant economic indicators: the weekly or monthly changes in commercial, industrial, and consumer loans, business production and inventories, the monetary aggregates (M1, M2 and M3), and so forth. The perpetual counterpoint that the Federal Reserve must play to avoid economic extremes (perhaps currently leading to "The Great Inflation of the 1990's") is always based on the subjective judgement of the Board of Governors. Fortunately, the private investor who wishes to gauge the likely future course of interest rates, and thus the likely future trend in the Dow, can rely on more than just the overt signs of widespread pessimism or general optimism[15] in anticipating counteractive decisions by the Federal Reserve: the Federal Funds rate on interbank overnight loans edges up or down

the Federal Funds rate

in advance of other rates influenced by Federal Reserve policy. Hence the trend in the *Federal Funds rate* should be followed on a weekly basis by prudent independent investors, for it is the most reliable barometer for predicting the future trend in the Dow.

According to cargo cult lore, certain *technical indicators* are supposed to forecast bull and bear markets for the Dow. Numerical quantities related to the character of trading on the NYSE and perhaps other exchanges, technical indicators may depend on the dollar amount of all stocks traded during the week, the dollar amounts of short sales (i.e., sales of borrowed stock) by various classes of traders, the number of issues advancing and the number declining in price during the week, the level of activity and sentiment manifest in stock option trading (i.e., contracts to buy or sell certain stocks at specified prices for prescribed periods of time), and other quantities that may change in magnitude with general market conditions in anteposition to the bull and bear market phases of the Dow. However, the structural roles played by market participants vary with

*technical
indicators*

time as a consequence of changes in group sentiment, demographics, technological and operational innovations, and other factors. Because of such structural changes in the make-up of the market, the appropriateness of formerly correlated technical indicators tends to fade with time. New and "improved" technical indicators are introduced occasionally by the cargo cultists,[16] but no set of technical indicators is likely to predict the future phases of the Dow with useful reliability owing to the dominant influence of the Federal Reserve and non-market factors that affect interest rate decisions.

"Thus in the beginning the world was so made that certain signs come before certain events."
—Cicero

seasonal predisposition for the Dow to go up or down

While technical indicators are often more misleading than reliable as predictors for future movements in the general market, there does exist an isochronal tendency for the Dow to trend upward during certain months of the year and to trend downward during other months, with a sufficient degree of correlation for the tendency to be weighted into trading decisions. This curious predisposition of the Dow for up movements during "favorable months" and down movements during "unfavorable months" may stem from the seasonality of business activity and the associated monthly variations in cash flow for institutional and private stock investment. In any event, the historically favorable and unfavorable months, arranged in order according to the degree of the statistical correlation, are respectively:

"Summer's lease hath all too short a date."
—Shakespeare

Favorable "Up" Months	Unfavorable "Down" Months
January (the best!)	October (the worst!)
August	May
December	June
July	February
March	November
April	September

On those sundry occasions when the Dow fails to conform to the historical pattern and moves the "wrong way" during one of the months, veteran traders are inclined to interpret the counteraction as a sign of latent and continuing weakness or strength in the general market. Thus for example, if the Dow trends downward during January, historical precedence suggests that one should anticipate unusual weakness throughout the first half of the year. Conversely, if the Dow advances during October, one can usually expect the market strength to carry through November as well as December.

"Cold autumn, wan with wrath of wind and rain."
—Swinburne

uncoupling from
the Dow

Providentially for investors, individual stocks often go through their own bullish and bearish phases in a manner that is essentially uncoupled from the Dow, with changes in α in Sharpe's equation on p. 144 dominating changes in $\beta \ln P_M$ for a period of several months (see footnote [1] on p. 130). Thus at any given time or phase in the Dow cycle, some stocks are excellent candidates for purchase while others should not be held. The companies whose stocks are most often uncoupled from the Dow are in businesses that are strongly affected by commodity price trends, foreign competition, and other factors more or less unrelated to the state of the general domestic economy. Examples of stock groups with members that are commonly in this uncoupled category are: Aluminum, Banks (NYC), Coal, Distilleries, Drugs, Farm Equipment, Forest Products, Gold and Silver, Grain Processing, Machine Tools, Metals (Misc.), Steel, Sugar, and Utilities. As a consequence of the fact that no two companies have the same product mix or the same dependence on commodity price trends and other international factors, the stocks in the groups stated above may or may not have major price movements that are unsynchronized with the Dow. That is, a stock must be considered on an individual basis and not as a group member if one wishes to determine whether uncoupling from the Dow is likely to occur.[17] In this regard it should be noted that a low P/E enhances a stock's ability to have a major upward price movement during any phase of the Dow, because a low P/E signifies a recent period of analyst-institutional neglect (see p. 139). An improving condition in analyst-institutional interest is usually signaled by positive *relative strength*,[18,19] evidenced by the stock holding firm on days when the Dow goes down and rallying on days when the Dow is nearly unchanged. Large-block institutional buying has become more passive since October 1987, and one can often detect imminent institutional accumulation *before* it happens on the NYSE. By asking a broker for a *quote and size* on a certain NYSE stock, you might get a response like, "$14\frac{1}{4}$ to $14\frac{3}{8}$, 25 by 30," where $14\frac{1}{4}$ is the bid price, the highest at which someone is willing to buy the stock, $14\frac{3}{8}$ is the asking

relative strength

quote and size

manifest
institutional
accumulation

price, the lowest at which someone is willing to sell the stock, and the remaining "25 by 30" is the so-called size, here meaning that 2500 shares are desired for purchase at $14\frac{1}{4}$ and 3000 shares are offered for sale at $14\frac{3}{8}$. When institutional accumulation enters, the size will be lopsided — something like "750 by 30." The combination of a low P/E, positive relative strength, and institutional accumulation can free a stock in a Dow bear market, especially if the stock is $sib+$ and P-V bullish.

panics

"This hypothesis
has put us in
a position to
establish
psychology upon
foundations
similiar to those
of any other
science, such as
physics."
—Freud

Finally, the psycho-sociological phenomenon of a general stock market *panic*, the sudden plummeting of the Dow and almost all NYSE stocks by a significant percentage in a single day of trading with very large concomitant volume, should be expected to occur naturally as a kind of *mass psychocatharsis* (Freudian guilt stemming from profits?) after a prolonged Dow bull market. Since many astute investors follow the course of interest rates as a precursor of trend reversal in the Dow, aggressive buying (characterized by sharp price rises on heavy volume) normally appears at the beginning of a Dow bull market, while aggres-

"If you still feel guilty about selling everything at the tops in 1987 and 1989, why not buy all of them back at the bottoms in the 1990's?"

sive selling (with sharp price drops on heavy volume) is evidenced at the onset of a Dow bear market. While it may or may not be instigated by rising interest rates and aggressive selling by astute investors, a panic in any case affords an excellent buying opportunity. If you are following a *sib+* stock and a panic occurs, you will often be able to obtain a position in the stock at a bargain price. Under no circumstance should any stock be sold during a panic, for prices are almost certain to recover and move up during the aftermath period.

a crash or superpanic

A supersized panic, or a confluence of several one-day panics, is now referred to generically as a *crash*. [20] Before October 1987 the most notorious stock market crash took place in October 1929 and signaled the end of the long Dow bull market that began more than five years earlier in 1924. This rush for the exits caused the Dow to fall precipitously by 30% from 330 to 230 in five days of hectic trading with record volume. In the aftermath period extending into 1930, the Dow rallied back to 295 before resuming its bear market downtrend, and those who did not sell during the crash of October 1929 were rewarded with more favorable price levels in the winter of 1929–1930.

In several respects the crash of October 1987 was remarkably similar to that of October 1929. Prior to either crash, the Dow had been in a prolonged five-year bull market with

a 1 : 3.5 increase in the stock price
index. In both cases the contempo-
rary technical indicators (see p. 149)
had not turned decisively negative
and signaled a Dow bear market
before the crash. Finally, the percentile drop in the Dow was approximately the same (about 30%) in
either case, when viewed over a
five-day time interval. Naturally the
Federal Reserve acted promptly to
halt this analogy after October 19,
1987.

*Octobers 1929
& 1987*

Historical precedence suggests
that panics will continue to occur
from time to time in the future
so long as auction stock markets
remain subject to human emotions
and/or computer "sell" programs!
While selective buying during a
panic is generally profitable, stocks
should only be sold after the panic
has transpired and if the individual
issues appear to be untimely to hold.

the future

NOTES

1. For example, informational asymmetry was usually the
   central ingredient in the amusing stories about Einstein
   that circulated years ago, like the following.
      Einstein advocated a bare minimum of personal pos-
   sessions because he was forgetful and lost practically
   everything. On a train trip in 1939 he went to the dining

car and realized that he had lost his reading glasses. He handed the little menu to the waiter and requested "Please read this to me." The waiter replied, "Boss, I is ignorant, too."

Upon arriving at his destination—a war relief banquet for Ethiopian refugees—Einstein was seated next to Greta Garbo. She said, "Herr Professor, I hope you can explain the theory of general relativity to me." Einstein replied that the theory of general relativity required some mathematical preliminaries, but he would be glad to explain the Newtonian theory of gravitation. He described how all bodies attract one another with a force proportional to the product of their masses divided by the square of their distance of separation, and how all bodies move in response to this gravitational force according to Newton's law of motion, (force) = (mass) × (acceleration). Greta listened very attentively until he had finished, thought for a moment, and then said "How long has this been going on?"

2. Morse, D., "Asymmetrical Information in Securities Markets and Trading Volume," *Journal of Financial and Quantitative Analysis*, Vol. 15, December 1980, pp. 1129–1148.

3. Grossman, S. J. and J. E. Stiglitz, "On the Impossibility of Informationally Efficient Markets," *American Economic Review*, Vol. 70, April 1980, pp. 393–408.

4. Diamond, D. W. and R. E. Verrecchia, "Information Aggregation in a Noisy Rational Expectation Economy," *Journal of Financial Economics*, Vol. 36, February 1981, pp. 221–235.

5. Jennings, R. H. and L. T. Starks, "Information Content and the Speed of Stock Price Adjustment," *Journal of Accounting Research,* Vol. 23, Spring 1985, pp. 336–350.

6. Bamber, L. S. "The Information Content of Annual Earnings Releases," *Journal of Accounting Research*, Vol. 24, Spring 1986, pp. 40–56.

7. Keynes, John Maynard, *The General Theory of Employment, Interest and Money*, London: Macmillan, 1949, p. 236.

8. This is one reason why the stocks of smaller companies are inefficient investment vehicles for private individuals. More important, the stock price movements of smaller companies fail to exhibit the predictable features evidenced by the stocks of larger (more visible, investment quality NYSE) companies.

9. Since many financial institutions systematically review every NYSE issue for possible purchase on a regular basis, one must assume that a NYSE company manifests decidedly undesirable features if only a few financial institutions own shares. A negligibly small institutional ownership may be reason enough to harbor doubts about the company's investment quality and to reject the stock as a candidate for purchase. As a prudent rule of thumb, one might require the stock to be held by no fewer than 25 institutions before admitting that it satisfies the investment quality requirement stated on pp. 88–91.

10. The problem is not unlike that of the professor who must simplify and condense two hours of material into a one-hour lecture because of a previous cancellation, say caused by heavy snow. This once happened to me, and the persistence of informational asymmetry was evident after my double lecture ended. "Are there any questions?" I asked. Following a long silence someone in my class raised a hand and posed the question: "Should we call to check for another lecture cancellation if there's another big snowfall?"

11. The sum total of a year's dividends in any common stock is insignificant when compared to the up and down price movement of the stock, and a year of dividends can always be eclipsed in a single day of price change. Nevertheless, dividends are a basic hallmark of quality — assurance that the earnings are genuine and the stock is longer-term investment grade.

12. A moderate or small long-term debt relative to the company's net worth (i.e., a small debt-to-equity ratio) is a practical measure of financial strength that can serve as an alternative to an S & P rating (see p. 89) for companies without publicly traded bonds. However, both a

decreasing long-term debt (viewed over a multi-year peri-od) and a decreasing number of shares outstanding (as effected by a corporate *buy-back program*) increase the attractiveness of a stock, as well as the likelihood of a *buyout* of the stock by insiders or others, so there are situations where an increasing debt-to-equity ratio may actually be beneficial.

13. The current *book value* of a common stock, defined as the estimated net liquidation worth of the company divided by the number of shares outstanding, is sometimes cited as an intrinsic measure of worth. Book value is stated as a single figure (without an estimated error) in S&P and Value Line stock reports, even though the computation of it involves numerous assumptions regarding the liqui-dation value of assets. (What is the value of the physical plant of a company if it cannot do business in a profitable and sustaining manner?) In the course of major up or down movements, the price of a stock may vary from a fraction to a multiple of its book value without useful correlation.

14. The Dow achieved a 1982–1987 bull market price ratio of about 1 : 3.5, but in a severe Dow bear market stocks can fall much faster and further than they can ever rise in a bull market: the Wall Street gravity principle— *Stocks can fall under their own weight*—is quite true. The capability of stocks to fall without let up was vividly illustrated in the worst Dow bear market, commencing in September 1929 (Dow at 383) and terminating in July 1932 (Dow at 41) to produce a 1929–1932 price ratio of about 9.3 : 1. It is profitable to hold most stocks in a Dow bull market, but it can be disastrous to hold most stocks in a major Dow bear market.

15. Optimism and pessimism derived from recent experience tend to produce bold and conservative psychologies in market traders. There is the illustrative story of the full service broker who had abandoned his conservative inhi-bitions in the 1982–1987 bull market to become a very successful speculator in margined call options. After gain-ing a large clientele, he lost everything in the Crash and

was pumping gas at an Exxon station in 1988. One day a former customer drove in and asked the broker for ten dollars of regular. "How far do you plan to go?" the broker asked. "To Scarsdale," his former customer replied. The broker did a quick mental calculation and said, "Well then, you'll only need two dollars worth of gas."

16. With each bull market there emerge new "prophets" who become forecasters of intermediate moves in the Dow, sometimes by invoking unfounded "theories" that are supposed to provide a basis for their insight. These self-annointed gurus are committed to a game of Russian roulette, in which their first or second well-publicized unlucky forecast is often their last.

17. To make sure that a major change in the business of the corporation has not taken place, one should check the text of a recent S&P or Value Line report.

18. Bohan, J., "Relative Strength: Further Positive Evidence," *Journal of Portfolio Management*, Fall 1981, pp. 36–39.

19. Brush, J., "Eight Relative Strength Models Compared," *Journal of Portfolio Mangement*, Fall 1986, pp. 21–28.

20. Ostensibly bad terminology, a *crash* suggests immobilization and finality and ignores the bounce. The term *super-panic* is much more apt.

5

SUPERIOR METHOD FOR STOCK INVESTMENTS

In his book that followed the crash of 1929 but preceded the advent of legally reported insider transactions, W. D. Gann[1] prescribed a list of "never-failing rules on stock selection and timing." The list of ten rules presented below actually retains some overlap with that of Gann, while incorporating a number of salutary operational principles in addition to the price-predictability findings and additional practical tenets discussed in the preceding chapters. While "never-failing" may be a trifle optimistic, "hardly ever-

"Those having torches will pass them on to others." —Plato

failing" is entirely appropriate, and the following ten rules provide the basis for a manifestly superior method for stock investments.

1. Concentrate exclusively on *sib*+ stocks so that imagery, informational asymmetry, and the analyst-institution symbiosis work for and not against you. By being exclusively *sib*+, your holdings will have the highest probability of price appreciation in any phase of the Dow cycle. To make your screening as timely as possible, subscribe to *Official Summary* (see footnote[8] on p. 108) and keep a composite list of *sib*+ stocks like the one shown in Table 4 on pp. 96-97.

subscribe to Official Summary and determine which stocks are sib+

2. Maintain P-V graphs for all current *sib*+ holdings and purchase candidates. As described in Chapter 3, P-V graphs are easy to construct and to keep up to date on a weekly basis. They are absolutely essential for the proper risk-averse timing of buy and sell transactions as well as for classifying the present risk inherent in a stock by the regime of motion displayed on its P-V graph (see pp. 125–130).

P-V graphs for sib+ stocks

3. Purchase a *sib*+ stock if it is P-V bullish and (1) the trend in interest rates favors a Dow bull market, or (2) the P-V bullish *sib*+ stock appears to have the capacity for a major upward price movement in a Dow bear market (see pp. 152–154). On the special occasion of a panic, a *sib*+ stock that is P-V bearish can be purchased if its price is well below the *sib* level.[2] Generally speaking, at any time in the economic cycle certain *sib*+ stocks qualify for purchase, with a high likelihood of favorable corporate developments and thus the potential for substantial price appreciation. As observed on p. 152, businesses that are less closely tied to the general domestic manufacturing and commercial sectors can have P-V bullish *sib*+ stocks that are predisposed to become uncoupled from the Dow and are therefore admissible for possible purchase at any time. However, if a Dow bull market appears imminent, purchases should be made preferentially of P-V bullish *sib*+ stocks that are *cyclical* in the usual sense of having an historically persistent coupling to the Dow.

when to purchase a sib+ stock

In cases for which a major price advance has occurred before you receive the *Official Summary* issue and become aware of the insider buying in a P-V bullish *sib*+ stock, it may or may not be advisable to wait for a pullback to within 10% of the *sib* price level before making a purchase. Here thoughtful deliberation must be applied on a stock-to-stock basis, with proper account taken of corporate news items that may have already impacted the stock price. In the absence of any such announcement of a favorable development, the rule is to buy immediately if the Dow is bullish or if the stock is likely to uncouple from a bearish Dow.

no news is good news

4. Sell a *sib*+ stock if (1) it has turned P-V bearish, or (2) insider selling is reported in *Official Summary*[3], or (3) the trend in interest rates favors a Dow bear market and the *sib*+ stock has already moved up more than 25% from your purchase price. The latter criterion for a sale is a quantification of Gann's dictum, "Never let a profit run into a loss," with the "greater than 25% appreciation" rule of thumb for selling a P-V bullish *sib+* stock in the final stage of a favorable general market indicated as an empirical risk-return trade-off.[4] While the tendency to sell *sib+* stocks prematurely should be resisted, most *sib+* stocks must be sold if a Dow bear market is likely to develop. In uncertain situations one should monitor the stock for a period of time with a quote and size (p. 153), and if a large offering appears to persist on the upper side of the quote, one should sell the stock at the bid price. Since Dow trend reversals are usually separated by at least several months, your strategic orientation based on timeliness relative to the Dow will change infrequently—only on those occasions when a change in the trend in interest rates signals the imminence of a Dow trend reversal.

when to sell a sib+ stock

5. Buy and sell exclusively with market orders, preferably at the opening, as soon as criteria for a buy or sell are evident. The independent investor has the principal advantage of being able to acquire or dispose of stock positions quickly, without committee approval or placement problems. To fully realize this advantage, one should always request a quote and size (p. 153) and buy at the asking price or sell at the bid price with a market order.[5] The volatility of the stock, the amount that you wish to buy or sell, the average daily volume, and the amount of stock in the size at both the bid and asking prices should of course always be considered in your buying and selling tactics. Transaction costs[6] are reduced substantially if buy and sell market orders are entered half an hour before the opening, when the bid-ask spread becomes zero by the matching of buy and sell orders and specialist intervention.

use only market orders, preferably at the opening

6. Be patient when no action is indicated, monitoring your holdings and purchase candidates on a weekly basis. Holding stocks in good companies for several months or years is one of the best forms of investment, and you should never sell a P-V bullish *sib*+ stock simply because the price has had a sizable advance, since purchase in a continuing Dow bull market. The equestrian but sound Wall Street adage is "Ride the winners." This was proper investment strategy even before the Tax Reform Act of 1986 repealed

buy and sell only when indicated, following your holdings on a weekly basis

the favorable long-term capital gains provision for Federal Income Tax, and now with long-term capital gains taxed in the same manner as ordinary income, there is even less sense in selling a stock that has performed well merely to nail down a profit. It is also important to be patient before buying a *sib+* stock, for the definition of P-V bullish on p. 116 requires the price to hold above its bear market nadir for a volume greater that ΔV *and* to commence an upward trend in which each successive intermediate decline holds at or above the previous intermediate low. If the price has held above the bear market nadir for a volume greater than ΔV but a significant upward movement from the nadir has not yet occurred, the stock is still said to be P-V bearish.

delay purchase until a sib+ stock is P-V bullish

A good Sunday newspaper with accurate NYSE price-volume figures is all you need to keep your P-V graphs up to date. In the case of a possible buy or sell situation you will of course follow your stock briefly on a daily basis with relevant input; however, checking all of your holdings or purchase candidates every day is more likely to produce impatience and investment inefficiency than to be helpful. Leave the perpetual torrent of financial data, rumors, opinions, and daily price volatility to the full-service brokers, advisory services, and their following.

7. Accumulate a surplus of investment funds in U.S. Treasury bills and bonds. After you have made a series of successful trades with $sib+$ stocks, you should put a fair part of your capital in Treasury securities (longer term Treasuries when 30-year bond yields are well above their recent five-year average, shorter term Treasuries at other times). This is an excellent counterweight to the tendency to become overconfident and careless with $sib+$ investments after a series of profitable selections. Treasury securities combine maximal safety and liquidity, and your reserve funds will be readily accessible for use at major bottoms in the Dow or for buying in a panic.

build up a surplus of investment funds in Treasury securities

8. Diversify modestly, to the extent that no less than 10% nor more than 20% of your investment capital is in any single stock. With every holding $sib+$

and timely, it is most efficient to put from 10% to 20% of your investment capital in any single stock. There may be periods during Dow bear markets when the cash in your money-market bank account plus your Treasury securities represents the greater part of your investment assets. Patience is required at such times and well rewarded later.

modest diversification, consistent with stringent selectivity

9. Have your account with a discount broker affiliated with a strong bank. Clearly a discount broker is the best place for your account with the independent method of stock investment described in this book. It is prudent to choose a discount broker affiliated with a strong bank in order to provide backup protection for the cash or securities in your account. Commission fees at full-service brokerage firms are standardly two or three times greater than those at a bank affiliated discount broker.[7] Moreover, full-service brokers are subject to a frenetic and overbearing flow of useless facts and figures (already incorporated into current stock prices) as well as rumor and misinformation. That many top-flight market profession-

use a discount broker

als insulate themselves from most of this noisy flow is well documented.[8]

Since a discount broker does not provide investment counseling, some investors miss the opportunity to discuss their buy, hold, and sell decisions with someone else. Indeed, it is true that such discussions can sharpen one's investment acumen and provide a psychological release from the uncertainties of stock ownership. Thus it may be worthwhile to have an investment partner who participates with you in the screening of the *Official Summary,* the maintenance of P-V graphs, and the other tasks involved in the stock investment method described here. Ideally, an investment partner should balance or complement one's own temperament with regard to bearing financial risk, in order to achieve an optimal combination of *daring conservatism* in your transactions.

10. Make it a cash account. Because there is adequate price movement in common stocks to satisfy the sensible investor without additional leverage, you should elect to have a basic cash account, pay

consider having an investment partner

daring conservatism, consistent with the method

"Debt is a prolific mother of folly."
—Disraeli

for your stocks in full, and have the stock certificates mailed to you in the venerable manner.[9] Assuming that you use a discount broker affiliated with a commercial bank, it is practical to tie your stock account to an FDIC-insured money-market-rate savings account at the bank, so that the required amounts for your stock purchases and the proceeds from your stock sales will be moved automatically from and to your bank account on settlement dates.

What makes stock investment such an interesting challenge is that a successful method may fade at any time and require a suitable revision to regain effectiveness. Since the ten rules above have engendered consistently profitable results during the past sixteen years, they provide a logical basis for a superior method of stock investment at the present time. However, it is important for the follower of a successful systematic method to view the subject as an artful science (somewhat analogous to the practice of internal medicine) and be willing to revise the method when evidence suggests the need for change. A receptiveness for signs of inefficiency and a willingness to

"They are not constants, but are changing still."
—Shakespeare

effect change accordingly is now more important than ever before, in light of the current pace of technological change in business, commerce, and the highly competitive arena of stock investments. With patient adherence to the method based on the ten rules above and a willingness to make appropriate modifications in the future if such are indicated by experience, the independent private investor should achieve a high level of success with his or her stock investments.

NOTES

1. Gann, William D., *Wall Street Selector,* New York: Financial Guardian, 1930.
2. The table below shows relevant price data for the second through the fifth *sib*+ entries on p. 96:

	average price of sib	12-month range before 10/19/87	panic low	recovery high through 10/28/88
BAC	$12\frac{1}{2}$	$10\frac{3}{8}$–$16\frac{1}{4}$	$7\frac{1}{2}$[b]	$18\frac{3}{8}$
BEL	$64\frac{1}{2}$	$61\frac{1}{2}$–$79\frac{3}{4}$	$60\frac{1}{2}$	77
KU	$18\frac{3}{4}$[a]	$16\frac{3}{4}$–$22\frac{1}{4}$	15	$20\frac{5}{8}$
GAF	46	$34\frac{1}{4}$–$69\frac{1}{2}$	$31\frac{3}{4}$	$56\frac{3}{8}$

[a] Adjusted for 2-for-1 split.
[b] Low of $5\frac{1}{4}$ in non-NYSE trading.

As is fairly typical for *sib*+ stocks, the average price of *sib* was in the lower part of the 12-month range for all four of these issues before the October panic. All four *sib*+ stocks recovered smartly after the panic, with an average percentile advance from the panic low to the subsequent recovery high of more than 65%.

3. See, for example, the discussion of GAF on pp. 98–99. Throughout this book the focus has been on holding long positions in *sib*+ stocks, but it is clear that short sales of stocks with significant *i*nsider *s*elling (*sis*) are also generally profitable. By definition, *sis* is the open market sale of over $100,000 worth of a company's stock by three or more insiders with no open market purchase of the stock during an *Official Summary* reporting period. An example of *sis* in mid-1987 appears on pp. 176-177 for illustrative purposes. The imminence or continuation of a major downtrend in the Dow (associated with rising interest rates) is the general precondition for shorting stocks.

4. A follower of the method may have purchased AVP on or about May 21, 1987, when *Official Summary* No. 2, Vol. 53 became available and revealed the *sib* (see pp. 30–31). By making such a prompt purchase, he or she would have been rewarded almost immediately, for after closing at $29\frac{3}{8}$ for the week ending May 22, AVP moved up rapidly in the following weeks and attained a new 12-month high of $38\frac{5}{8}$ during the week ending August 14, rising that week for a net change of only $+\frac{5}{8}$ on volume of 4,145,000 shares. The latter abnormally large volume (more than twice the average weekly volume during the preceding three months) and relatively small price change of $+\frac{5}{8}$ signaled the beginning of a P-V top to the 31.5% rise in the stock price in three months. The sale of AVP at about 38 on Monday, August 17, was clearly indicated by the abnormal price-volume activity during the preceding week, the bearish outlook for the Dow produced by rising interest rates, and the "greater than 25% appreciation rule" for taking profits in such situations.

Example of *sis,* significant insider selling (see note 3 on p. 175)

OFFICIAL SUMMARY OF

ISSUER
  SECURITY
    REPORTING PERSON
      NATURE OF OWNERSHIP
	Relationship	Date of trans-action	Character	Late, amended or inconsistent

AMES DEPT STORES INC				
COM				
BARBATO JOHN RICHARD	O			
DIRECT		06/24/87	S	L
INDIRECT		07/13/87		
BLASSBERG STEVEN J	O			
DIRECT		07/10/87	S	
CALOGINE JOSEPH	O			
DIRECT		06/29/87	X	L
LARIVIERE LAWRENCE LEWIS	O			
DIRECT		07/23/87	X	
SHAPIRO STUART J	O			
DIRECT		07/01/87	S	
INDIRECT		07/23/87		
MINK ALAN R	O			
INDIRECT		07/10/87	S	

SECURITY TRANSACTIONS AND HOLDINGS

TRANSACTIONS				Month end holdings of securities
Bought or otherwise acquired		Sold or otherwise disposed of		
Amount	Price	Amount	Price	
		1,000	$24.13	1,666
				292
		1,400	$25.00	
1,200	$11.13			2,400
17	$4.34			1,857
		2,044	$23.63	10,983
				5,440
		686	$24.88	300

5. Since *sib*+ stocks are by definition certain actively traded NYSE issues, the use of market orders is especially appropriate for them. *Limit orders,* with a prefixed price at which you would like to buy or sell, are pennywise and pound foolish and should never be used. In addition to the main drawback of permitting the stock to move away from the limit price without an execution, a buy limit order gives the market a *free put option* (your contract to buy at the limit price) that can be executed on unfavorable news by aggressive selling, while a sell limit order gives the market a *free call option* (your contract to sell at the limit price) that can be executed on favorable news by aggressive buying. Hence whether executed or not, a limit order can work to the disadvantage of the user. Even less desirable is the *open limit order* (or GTC, for "good till cancelled"), which stays in place for an indefinite period of time as a free call or put option for all other market participants.

6. Provided the order is of a size that does not move the market, the *transaction cost* for buying or selling a certain amount of stock is defined as the brokerage commission plus one-half the spread between the bid and asking prices, because active buying or selling usually occurs at the asking or bid price, respectively:

$$\text{(transaction cost)} = \text{(brokerage commission)} + \tfrac{1}{2}\,[\text{(asking price)} - \text{(bid price)}]$$

Many small-capitalization stocks on NASDAQ and the AMEX have large spreads between the bid and asking prices, and the excessive transactions costs involved in buying and selling such issues further impair their appropriateness for private investors. For interesting recent discussions of how transaction costs can alter the profitability of stock investments, see Perold, André F., "The Implementation Shortfall: Paper versus Reality," *Journal of Portfolio Management,* Spring 1988, pp. 4–9; Sweeney, Richard J., "Some New Filter Rule Tests: Methods and Results," *Journal of Financial and Quantitative Analysis,* Vol. 23, September 1988, pp. 285–300.

7. Three discount brokerage firms with strong bank affilia-
tion and offices in the Philadelphia area are listed below.
Representative buy or sell commissions for a stock priced
at $30 per share are also shown, to provide some informa-
tive current benchmarks:

	100 shares @ $30/ sh	500 shares @ $30/ sh	1000 shares @ $30/ sh
CoreStates Securities (Philadelphia National Bank)	$56	$140	$185
Fidelcor Brokerage (Fidelity Bank)	$50	$130	$180
TradeSaver (Provident National Bank)	$55	$105	$120

8. For example, see Grieves, Robin, and J. Clay Singleton,
"Analytic Methods of the All-American Research Team,"
Journal of Portfolio Management, Fall 1987, pp. 20–24.
9. There are several good reasons why it is not advisable to
leave your stock in your brokerage account. First, with
legal transfer and possession of the stock certificates, your
name will automatically be added to the corporate list of
shareholders, and you will receive reports, proxy state-
ments and other stockholder communications regularly
and directly. Second, your stock will not be available for
use in short sales, as is sometimes done with *street name*
(i.e., brokerage account) positions. Third, your stock will
not be subject to the unwarranted risk of a sudden financial problem at your brokerage firm or at another firm that
has borrowed your stock for a short sale. Finally, you will
be less inclined to sell your stock prematurely if the actual
certificates reside in your safe deposit box. There should
not be any additional fee to receive your stock certificates,
since this service is already figured in the brokerage firm's
commission schedule.

APPENDIX: AN *"OFFICIAL SUMMARY"* OF THE METHOD, BY WAY OF EXAMPLE

As a synopsis of the superior method for selecting, purchasing, monitoring, and eventually selling a stock, let us go through the entire procedure in chronological sequence for an actual recent example with a short-term holding period.

Friday, November 25, 1988. You receive No. 9, Vol. 54 of *Official Summary* in the mail, and your customary monthly perusal reveals about a dozen *sib* stocks (i.e., those with significant insider buying). By using a recent *Standard & Poor's Stock Guide,* you eliminate about half of the *sib* stocks as non-NYSE, or if on the NYSE as lacking adequate *visibility* (indicated by a trading volume averaging less than 100,000 shares/week) or *investment quality* (suggested if fewer than 25 institutions hold the stock). Among those that survive this initial screening is the ordinary stock (stoque ordinaire, si préférez vous!), meaning "common" in our parlance, of the large transportation conglomerate to the north, Canadian Pacific (CP), with the *Official Summary sib* entry shown on p. 184–187. The following pertinent information appears for CP in the *S & P Stock Guide* for October 1988:

Ticker Symbol	Name of Issue	Market	Inst. Hold Cos.	Sept. Sales in 100's
CP	Canadian Pacific	NY,...	342	75912

Copyright © Standard & Poor's, 1988.

Saturday, November 26, 1988.
You spend time in a library that subscribes to *S & P* and *Value Line* stock reports to learn more about

the current NYSE *sib* stocks that
are likely to have adequate visibility and hence have passed your initial screening of the recent *Official
Summary* issue. At this point you
first confirm that the stock is covered
by *Value Line* (to insure adequate
visibility), and then you concentrate
on *investment quality* as a filter
device: you wish to eliminate any
sib stock that has publicly traded
bonds rated CCC or lower or a long-
term debt significantly greater than
the company's equity (net worth). In
particular, Canadian Pacific is covered by *Value Line,* and the company's publicly traded bonds carry
the *S & P* rating of AA. Moreover,
Canadian Pacific's moderate debt-to-
equity ratio (less than one, i.e., debt
smaller than net worth) has declined
in every year since 1982, a long-
term trend which greatly enhances
the company's attractiveness. You
also note that CP has a relatively
low price-to-earnings ratio, a P/E
about equal to 7.6 (for P = US$16.75
and E = C$2.60 with C$1.00 = US
85¢); the low P/E indicates that this
stock is relatively unpopular with
the analysts and the institutions,
even though the number of institutions holding CP in their portfolios

(From No. 9 of Vol. 54, received by subscribers on or about November 25, 1988)

OFFICIAL SUMMARY OF

ISSUER
  SECURITY
    REPORTING PERSON
      NATURE OF OWNERSHIP
	Relationship	Date of trans-action	Character	Late, amended or inconsistent

COM				
HOLLYWOOD CAMERA CARS INC	B			
INDIRECT		07/01/88	U	
NEEDHAM HAL	D			
DIRECT		07/08/88	H	
INDIRECT		07/01/88	T	
CAMPEAU CORP				
P				
COM				
OLYMPIA & YORK DEV. LTD	B			
DIRECT		08/29/88	P	
CANADIAN OCCIDENTAL PETE LTD				
COM				
THORPE BRIAN D	O			
DIRECT		08/10/88	X	
CANADIAN PAC LTD				
ORO				
DEGROOTE MICHAEL G	D			
DIRECT		08/08/88	3	
INDIRECT		08/08/88	3	

SECURITY TRANSACTIONS AND HOLDINGS

| TRANSACTIONS | | | | Month end holdings of securities |
| Bought or otherwise acquired | | Sold or otherwise disposed of | | |
Amount	Price	Amount	Price	
		20,000		1,092,500
		20,000		45,020
20,000				1,092,500
555,576	$16.57			4,732,286
8,900	$13.88			8,900
				2,000
				12,000,000

OFFICIAL SUMMARY OF

ISSUER
  SECURITY
    REPORTING PERSON
      NATURE OF OWNERSHIP
	Relationship	Date of trans-action	Character	Late, amended or inconsistent

DODGE EDWIN V	O			
INDIRECT		08/26/88	P	
FATT WILLIAM ROBERT	C			
DIRECT		08/12/88	P	
DIRECT		08/12/88	P	A
DIRECT		08/17/88	P	
DIRECT		08/17/88	P	A
KINGSMILL ARDAGH S	D			
DIRECT		08/11/88		
INDIRECT		07/29/88	P	
MICHALS GEORGE F	O			
DIRECT		08/23/88	P	
ORD PAR #5				
RITCHIE ROBERT JAMIESON	O			
DIRECT		08/12/88	U	
DIRECT		08/25/88	P	
INDIRECT		08/12/88	T	
CONS PREF 4%				
FIELDING MALCOLM J	D			
INDIRECT		07/19/88	P	L
INDIRECT		07/27/88	P	L
INDIRECT		07/28/88	P	L

SECURITY TRANSACTIONS AND HOLDINGS

TRANSACTIONS				Month end holdings of securities
Bought or otherwise acquired		Sold or otherwise disposed of		
Amount	Price	Amount	Price	
4,300	$21.13			5,000
2,000	$22.00			
2,000	$22.00			
2,000	$22.25			4,000
2,000	$22.25			4,000
				19,783
3,300	$22.50			3,300
5,000	$21.50			5,000
		1		
500				555
				1
6,500	$1.05			
18,200	$1.05			
8,800	$1.05			8,708,051

Total amount of Canadian Pacific *sib* during period: US$412,000. [Note that the purchase prices shown in the *Official Summary* listing for CP are stated in Canadian dollars (pertaining to transactions made on the Montreal or Toronto Exchanges) with C$1 = US85¢.]

has increased substantially in recent years:

S&P Stock Guide issue	March '86	April '87	Oct. '88
No. institutions holding CP	172	233	342

Copyright © Standard & Poor's, 1986-1988.

Notwithstanding the fact that the company is involved in the production of certain commodities (namely, oil, gas, coal, and forest products), the long-term price chart in either the *S & P* or *Value Line* stock report shows that CP is essentially *cyclical*, that is, fairly well-coupled to the Dow. The most recent immediate top for this stock occurred in July 1988.

Sunday, November 27, 1988. You include CP in the set of *sib*+ stocks to be monitored with P-V graphs. By using your collection of NYSE pages from Sunday newspapers running back to July, you construct the P-V graph for CP shown on p. 189. The selloff volume $\Delta V = 12.23$ is evident on this graph, with the slight fractional penetrations of 16 at $V = 28.75$ and $V = 30.10$ viewed as successful tests of the nadir of the decline: $16\frac{1}{8}$ at

Figure 13.   CP from 7/5/88 to 11/25/88 (ΔV = 12.23 from $19\frac{7}{8}$ to $16\frac{1}{8}$)

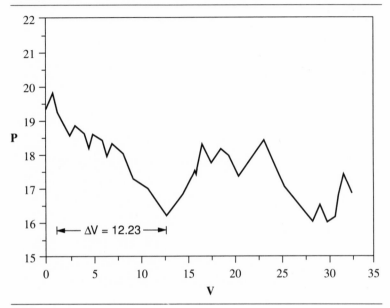

$V = 12.85$. Hence, CP has already turned P-V bullish, because a volume greater than ΔV has transpired *after* the decline ended and the stock has rallied significantly (i.e., back to $18\frac{1}{2}$) in the course of this consolidation.

Although CP is *sib*+ and P-V bullish, your decision to purchase this stock must hinge on the likely near term trend of the Dow, because CP is essentially cyclical and prone to decline in a Dow bear market. You observe the bearish tone in the Federal Funds rate, which has been edging up in recent months and is currently at 8.45%. However, December is traditionally a favorable "up" month for the Dow, and January (the best historically) is often an outstanding "up" month. On the basis of the favorable seasonality for cyclical stocks in December and January, you decide to buy CP immediately.

Monday, November 28, 1988.
You telephone your discount broker before 9:00 a.m. New York time and place an order to buy CP at the opening. The stock opens at $16\frac{3}{4}$, which is therefore your purchase price, with the Dow at 2075.

December 1988 and January 1989. Owing in part to the Dow's favorable behavior, CP moves up strongly in the typical P-V bullish *sib+* manner during December and January. You continue to follow Canadian Pacific entries in *Official Summary*, and you note additional insider buying in No. 10, Vol. 54 (on pages 192-193) and again in No. 11, Vol. 54 (on pages 194-195).

Sunday, February 5, 1989. You update your P-V graph for CP and obtain Figure 14 shown on p. 196. [In order to display the entire relevant price-volume relation from 7/5/88 to 2/3/89, note that the V scale has been compressed in the longer-term P-V graph on p. 196 relative to the shorter-term P-V graph on p. 189]. Closing right at the new 12-month high of $21\frac{1}{4}$ on Friday, February 3, after a fairly steep (hence rather bearish) *oscillation-convection* that has run for ten weeks, Canadian Pacific has advanced nearly 27% from your purchase price of $16\frac{3}{4}$ in late November. The Federal Funds rate has now moved decisively above 9%, increasing the likelihood of a decline in the Dow. Moreover, the Dow has an historical predisposition to trend downward in February. Because it is most likely to go down during a period of weakness in the general market, CP must be sold.

Monday, February 6, 1989. You call your broker before 9:00 a.m. New York time and place an order to sell CP at the opening. The stock opens at $21\frac{1}{8}$, which is therefore your sale price, with the Dow at 2331. If the discount broker's commissions and a dividend payment

OFFICIAL SUMMARY OF

ISSUER
  SECURITY
    REPORTING PERSON
      NATURE OF OWNERSHIP
	Relationship	Date of trans-action	Character	Late, amended or inconsistent

CANADIAN PAC LTD				
ORO				
FIELDING MALCOLM J	D			
DIRECT		09/15/88		
INDIRECT		08/30/88	P	L
INDIRECT		08/31/88	P	L
INDIRECT		09/01/88	P	
INDIRECT		09/02/88	P	
CON PREF 4%				
FIELDING MALCOLM J	D			
DIRECT		09/15/88		
INDIRECT		08/09/88	P	L
INDIRECT		08/16/88	P	L
INDIRECT		08/18/88	P	L
INDIRECT		08/30/88	P	L
STERLING PREF 4%				
FIELDING MALCOLM J	D			
DIRECT		09/15/88		
INDIRECT		08/30/88	P	L

SECURITY TRANSACTIONS AND HOLDINGS

TRANSACTIONS				Month end holdings of securities
Bought or otherwise acquired		Sold or otherwise disposed of		
Amount	Price	Amount	Price	
				51,300
900	$21.00			
368,857	$20.95			2,606,347
232,800	$20.95			
181,700	$20.95			3,020,847
				40,200
1,500	$1.05			
4,000	$1.05			
3,000	$1.05			
1,500	$1.10			8,718,051
				10,800
1,943	$0.98			1,911,504

OFFICIAL SUMMARY OF

ISSUER
  SECURITY
    REPORTING PERSON
      NATURE OF OWNERSHIP
	Relationship	Date of trans-action	Character	Late, amended or inconsistent

CANADIAN PAC LTD				
ORD				
MACNAUGHTON ANGUS A	D			
DIRECT		10/07/88	P	
ORD PAR $5				
MACNAUGHTON ANGUS A	D			
DIRECT		09/09/88	P	
RITCHIE ROBERT JAMIESON	O			
DIRECT		10/04/88	T	
INDIRECT		10/04/88	U	

SECURITY TRANSACTIONS AND HOLDINGS

Bought or otherwise acquired		Sold or otherwise disposed of		Month end holdings of securities
TRANSACTIONS				
Amount	Price	Amount	Price	
2,500	$21.75			25,000
12,500	$20.37			22,500
1				557
		1		

Figure 14. CP from 7/5/88 to 2/3/89 (ΔV = 12.23 from $19\frac{7}{8}$ to $16\frac{1}{8}$)

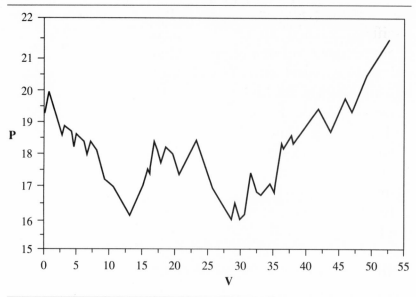

(received in January) are taken into account, your net investment return is approximately 26%, more than twice the 12.3% gain in the Dow (as it advanced from 2075 to 2331) during your ten-week holding period.

Epilogue: Due to the continuing rise in the Federal Funds rate, February 1989 was indeed an unfavorable "down" month for the Dow, and nearly all cyclical stocks (including CP) suffered significant declines. The weakness in CP continued until mid-May, when the nadir of the decline was reached at 18. During the following six weeks, Canadian Pacific remained above 18, traded a cumulative volume greater than $\Delta V = 12.23$, and turned P-V bullish once again in late June at 19. An easing in the Federal Funds rate and a strong Dow spurred CP to advance in a $sib+$ P-V bullish fashion during July and achieve the new 12-month high of 24 on Monday, July 31. Interestingly, the timing of the latter price peak closely followed the July 28 reception date for subscribers of *Official Summary* Vol. 55, No. 5, which reported the $112 million open market *sale* of 6 million CP shares by a director.

INDEX